THE WI BOOK OF — CAKES

JILL BRAND

WI BOOKS

Copyright © National Federation of Women's Institutes
First Published 1999 by WI Books

in association with Stable Ltd
Glebe House, Church Street,
Crediton, Devon EX17 2AF

Illustrated by Michael Lye

British Library Cataloguing in Publication Data.
A CIP catalogue record for this book is available from the British Library.

ISBN 0947990 72 0

Printed and bound in Great Britain by Short Run Press Ltd, Exeter, Devon

Note for Showing
If you are intending to use any of the recipes in this book for Schedules for Shows, remember to consult an up-to-date copy of *On With the Show*.

CONTENTS

INTRODUCTION   **6**

Cake Making   6

Problems Chart   9

Guide to Perfect Baking   10

Fats and Oils   11

Using Fats and Oils (chart)   12

What is Unrefined Sugar?   13

FRUIT CAKES   **14**

My Favourite Fruit Cake   14

Apple and Walnut Cake   15

Paradise Cake   15

Apricot, Prune and Cherry Cake   16

Golden Christmas Cake   16

Semi-Rich Fruit Cake   17

Dundee Cake   17

Chairman's Cake   18

Golden Harvest Cake   18

Guinness Cake   19

Christmas Cake   20

Modern Christmas Cake   20

Sunshine Fruit Cake   21

Simnel Cake   22

Mauritian Easter Cake   23

Irish Tea Brack   23

Date and Walnut Cake   24

Half Pound Cake   24

Highland Fruit Cake   24

Marmalade & Courgette Cake   25

Boiled Fruit Cake   25

LARGE CAKES   **26**

Banana Butterscotch Cake   26

Cherry Cake   27

Cherry and Almond Cake   28

Old Fashioned Seed Cake   28

Coffee and Almond Cake   29

Lemon and Cardamom Cake   29

Lemon and Ginger Cake   30

Coconut Cake   30

Lemon Drizzle Cake   31

Rich Almond Cake   31

Passion Cake   32

Simple Ginger Cake   32

Sandcake   33

Rum and Orange Cake   34

Spiced Honey Cake   34

Snow White Cake   35

Parkin   36

Sticky Gingerbread   36

St Clement's Cake   37

Peach and Almond Cake   37

CONTENTS

TEA LOAVES 38

Apple Tea Bread 38
Banana Tea Loaf 39
Cranberry and Apricot Tea Bread 39
Date and Cherry Tea Loaf 40

Date and Walnut Tea Bread 40
Spiced Plum Tea Bread 41
Tropical Fruit Tea Loaf 42
Mixed Fruit Tea Loaf 42

CHOCOLATE 43

All-in-One Chocolate Cake 43
Chewy Chocolate Squares 44
Mocha Cake 44
Chocolate Almond Brownies 45
Chocolate and Banana Cake 46
Orange Chocolate Drizzle Cake 46
Dark Chocolate Cake 47

Death by Chocolate Fudge Cake 48
Coconut and Chocolate Crunch 49
Light Chocolate Cake 49
Fudgy Chocolate Loaf 50
Rich Chocolate Cake 50
Traditional American Brownies 51
Sachertorte 52

SMALL CAKES 53

Macaroons 53
Gingerbread Hollows 53
Chocolate Cup Cakes 54
Swiss Whirls 54
Coconut Buns 55
Lemon Butterfly Cakes 55

Madeleines 56
Raspberry Buns 56
Mini Passion Cakes 57
Rock Cakes 58
Small Cakes 58

MISCELLANEOUS 59

Coffee Pecan Bars 59
Cherry and Apricot Scones 60
Scones 60
Orange and Lemon Bars 61

Apricot and Coconut Bars 61
Tea Time Fruity Squares 62
Ginger Slice 62

CONTENTS

TRADITIONAL 63
Victoria Sandwich 63
All-in-One Victoria Sandwich 63
Coffee and Walnut Cake 64

Sponge Cakes 64
Swiss Roll 65

LINING A CAKE TIN 66

CHARTS 66
Temperature Conversion Chart 66
Special Occasions Cakes 67
Wedding Cakes 67
Special Occasions Cake Chart 68–69
Madeira Cake and Chart 70–71
Lining a Deep Cake Tin 70
Moist Chocolate Cake and Chart 72–73
Buttercream 72

INGREDIENTS INDEX 74–78

ABOUT THE WI 79

ABOUT THE AUTHOR 79

BILLINGTONS
The Unrefined Sugar Experts 80

INTRODUCTION

Successful cake making involves your time and energy. Before using the recipes in this book, spare a little time to read the introduction and the guidelines given. It could save a lot of heartache later.

CAKE MAKING

It is thought that cake making probably evolved from early pastry making. Pastry was a simple paste of flour and water that protected meat from direct heat used in cooking. The mixture of juices and dripping from the meat helped create the first true pastry. Early cakes and buns were first a doughy mixture with dried fruit, berries and spices added – often to use up pastry scraps prior to fasting or to celebrate after a period of religious observance, such as Lent – hence the Easter breads and cakes made throughout Europe. Cakes were also a way of making use of preserved fruits, citrus rinds, nuts and seeds. Sometimes sweet and savoury ingredients were mixed, as in earliest mince pies. Precious spices from the East helped preserve meat and gradually cooks evolved ways of making a particular flavour the central theme of a cake.

Cakes are basically made from fat, flour, sugar and eggs, with the exception of the sponge, which is fatless. The texture varies according to the method of preparation and the proportion of fat to flour. The richest cakes include equal proportions of the basic ingredients as in a Victoria Sandwich.

THE 'ALL-IN-ONE' METHOD

This is a quick and easy way of preparing all types of cakes.

All the ingredients are beaten together and air is incorporated into the mixture to form air cells which are stabilised by sugar. By using softened or whipped types of fat, air is easily incorporated and the other ingredients mix quickly.

Additional raising agent should be added as not enough air will be introduced during the mixing process. During baking, the fat melts and the raising agent reacts with the liquid from the egg to produce carbon dioxide and steam. As pressure builds up inside the cake, these gases are transferred to the air cells formed during mixing and allow the cake to rise. By the end of baking, the proteins in the flour and eggs are set. The cooked cake consists of a large number of air cells surrounded by proteins in which starch granules are held.

The texture of a cake made by using the 'All-in-One' method is fairly open.

THE 'CREAMING' METHOD

This is the most traditional method of cake making.

The fat and sugar are beaten together until the mixture is light in colour, fluffy in texture and the sugar has been incorporated. A large number of air cells are produced which are stabilised by the sugar. Additional air cells are introduced by beating the eggs into the mixture. So that no air is lost, the sieved flour should be folded in gently, using a metal spoon in a cutting motion. During baking the cake rises for the same reasons as the 'All-in-One' cake.

The texture of a cake made by the 'Creaming' method is a closer and finer than an 'All-in-One' cake.

THE 'RUBBING-IN' METHOD

This method is used for cakes usually with half or less than half fat to flour. The fat is cut into fairly small pieces and rubbed lightly into the flour with the fingertips and thumbs. At the same time the mixture should be lifted well above the bowl to help incorporate air into the cake until the mixture resembles fine breadcrumbs.

The texture of a cake made by the 'Rubbing-In' method is fairly open.

THE 'MELTING' METHOD

This is a very easy method of preparing cakes, as a minimum amount of handling is required. It is the traditional method for preparing Gingerbread.

The fat, sugar, syrup, liquid and fruit (if used) are heated gently until melted. (Take care not to overheat the ingredients.) The mixture is cooled and added to the dry ingredients and then beaten together with the egg until well mixed.

The texture of Gingerbread is fairly open and that of a Fruit Cake fairly crumbly but both are moist.

THE 'WHISKING' METHOD

This is method used for preparing fatless sponges, Swiss rolls and also Genoese Sponges.

Traditionally the eggs and sugar are whisked together for 10–15 minutes over hot water to dissolve the sugar completely and then for a further 5 minutes off the heat to cool the mixture. A great deal of air is incorporated into the mixture at this stage to give the cake its light, spongy texture. Finally, the sieved flour is folded in very carefully so that the incorporated air is not lost.

Note: If using an electric mixer, the whisking time will be reduced to 5–10 minutes and it will not be necessary to whisk over hot water.

The texture of a fatless sponge is even, light and very soft. It dries out very quickly and so should be eaten within 2 days of baking.

BAKING WITH OIL

Making cakes with oil saves time as there is no creaming or rubbing-in.

Cakes made in this way turn out less rich in taste and lighter in colour than those made with butter or margarine. They need extra baking powder as less air can be incorporated into an oil mixture. For cakes, add extra baking powder – 5 ml (1 level teaspoon) to 115–140 g (4–5 oz) self raising flour. The cakes have an open texture and tend to be more crumbly and a little less moist.

It is important to grease the cake tin before lining with parchment or grease-proof paper, then grease the paper and dust with flour.

STORAGE

All cakes must be quite cold before storing, otherwise mould will develop. Cakes keep best in a clean, airtight tin. A sponge should be eaten within two days, a Victoria Sandwich will keep up to a week, a Rich Fruit cake will keep for months in a completely airtight tin. Alternatively, cakes can be wrapped in double greaseproof paper, then in a sheet of foil, and stored in a cool dry place.

PROBLEMS	ALL-IN-ONE MIXTURE	CREAMED MIXTURE	WHISKED MIXTURE
Hollow top	Overbeating. Too cool an oven. Insufficient cooking. Fat become too soft.	Over creaming of mixture. Too cool an oven. Insufficient cooking. Too much raising agent.	
Domed top	Oven temp. too high, adjust temp. Cake baked too high in oven, adjust shelf position.	Oven temp. too high, adjust temp. Cake baked too high in oven, adjust shelf position.	Oven temp. too high, adjust temp. Cake baked too high in oven, adjust shelf position.
Close, damp texture	Insufficient cooking.	Insufficient creaming. Too much liquid, too little flour, too much sugar.	Insufficient whisking. Insufficient cooking. Ingredients not measured correctly.
Coarse texture	Too much raising agent	Too much raising agent. Flour unevenly mixed.	
Collar edge on baked cake	Cake has risen too rapidly and sunk – cake baked too high in oven, adjust shelf, too much raising agent, check proportion. Fan oven preheated.	Cake has risen too rapidly and sunk – cake baked too high in oven, adjust shelf, too much raising agent, check proportions.	
Sugar spotting		Insufficient creaming, sugar still undissolved.	
Too shallow, not risen			Insufficient whisking. Too cool an oven. Insufficient raising agent.
Wrinkling on top, after baking			Slightly under-cooked. Tin too small, use next size of tin.
Risen unevenly	Mixture unevenly spread in tin. Oven shelves not level, adjust using spirit level.	Mixture unevenly spread in tin. Oven shelves not level, adjust using spirit level.	Flour not folded in properly. Mixture unevenly spread in tin. Oven shelves not level, adjust using spirit level.

GUIDE TO PERFECT BAKING

Cakes and Sponges

1. A good light cake relies on air being incorporated into the mixture during the making. When making a cake by the 'All-in-One' method, baking powder is used as well as self raising flour. This is necessary – no air is incorporated during the mixing as in the case of the traditional 'Creaming' method.

2. Always bake sponge cakes as soon as they are mixed. This is especially important with those that use baking powders as a raising agent, as this starts to work as soon as it comes into contact with moisture. (Very rich fruit cakes can be left for a few hours before baking – important if you are making a large wedding cake and can't fit all the tiers in your oven at the same time.)

3. Take care to weigh all ingredients carefully to ensure the proportions are right.

4. Remember, when cooking sponges and cakes in a fan oven, that the temperature should be reduced by 20°C, 70°F and the oven does not need pre-heating. All the recipes in this book have fan oven temperatures.

5. To avoid the cakes sinking NEVER open the oven door during the early part of cooking; try to avoid opening the oven door until at least half the recommended time has elapsed.

Baking

Oven temperatures in this book are just guidelines, as every oven is slightly different. Most consumers know their own oven's characteristics and you may need to adjust the temperatures by up to 15°C, 60°F or 1 Gas Mark. The recipes do not give shelf positions as, again, ovens vary as a general rule

Fan ovens: Due to the even heat distribution, shelf positions are not important.

Conventional electric ovens and **Gas ovens:** When baking cakes in shallow tins or on baking trays, they should be positioned on shelves evenly spaced in the oven. Always remember that the cakes at the top will cook quicker and the lower ones will need additional cooking time and moving to the higher position.

When baking larger cakes they should be baked on the middle or below centre shelves – always consult the oven manufacturer's handbook for guidance.

You may find it necessary to cover the top of rich deep cakes to avoid overbrowning, carefully place a sheet of greaseproof paper over the top of the cake.

Cooling

If you allow the cake to cool in the tin for the time suggested in the recipe, it will be firmer and easier to handle. When a cake has a light, fragile top, turn it out onto a cooling rack covered with a clean tea towel, cover with another cooling rack and immediately invert both racks together and remove the top rack. This also avoids marking the top, which is important if entering cakes in a show for judging.

FATS AND OILS

This information is to ensure you can choose the best products to use for baking.

What is the difference between a fat and an oil?

The term fat is used to describe a product that remains solid at room temperature. The most familiar fats are those derived from animals – butter, lard, suet and dripping. Fats are used for spreading and cooking.

Oils are the refined end product of a nut or seed-crushing process, and are mostly used for cooking, deep frying, stir frying and salad dressing, as they remain liquid at room temperature.

In addition to basic fats and oils, today there is a wide variety of margarines and spreads to choose from. Spreads vary in their fat content; this affects not only their nutritional value but also their cooking performance.

What products should I buy for best baking results?

Margarine was first formulated about 90 years ago and came onto the UK market 70 years ago. During the Second World War, margarine was the universal alternative to butter and has enjoyed a special place on the family table ever since. A full fat margarine, containing not less than 80% fat, will perform spreading and cooking in a similar way to butter. It is today largely used for family cooking and baking.

Hard Margarines are made with a blend of hydrogenated fish and vegetable oils. The blend is perfect for baking, particularly for traditional methods – that is the 'Rubbing-in' method of pastry making and 'Creaming' for cakes. Before creaming, hard margarine can be allowed to soften for a short time at room temperature. Hard margarines give more reliable results in rich fruit cakes by giving more support to the cake structure, and so an even distribution of fruit.

Soft Margarines are made with a blend of hydrogenated oils, specially blended to give a softer consistency. They should be used straight from the refrigerator for cooking. For the most reliable results, the 'All-in-One' method of cake making is recommended. You can use soft margarines for all types of cakes.

Packet Spreads perform well in traditional cake and pastry making and, like hard margarines, are an alternative to butter.

Tub Spreads are best used straight from the refrigerator. They are excellent used in the 'All in One' method of cake making. Tub spreads are not recommended for rich fruit cakes.

USING FATS AND OILS

	SPREADING	CAKES	ICINGS	FRUIT CAKES
Block margarine	yes	yes	yes	yes
Soft tub margarine	yes	yes	yes	yes
Spreads	yes	yes	no	semi-rich fruit cakes only
Low fat spread	yes	scones, plain cakes	no	no
Very low fat spread	yes	no	no	no
White fat	no	strongly flavoured only	no	lacking flavour
Cooking oils	no	yes	no	yes

WHAT IS UNREFINED SUGAR?

The distinction between unrefined brown sugars and refined brown sugars comes from the way sugar cane is processed. Unlike *refined* brown sugars, which are really white sugar with a colour coating, *unrefined* golden and brown sugars are produced with the aim of locking in – rather than refining out – the natural molasses present in the sugar cane. Even better, unrefined sugar is a healthier option than white sugar as it contains the natural goodness of minerals such as iron and calcium along with trace elements. White sugar loses its flavour in the refining process, as the valuable molasses is removed – leaving just concentrated sweetness.

The range of unrefined sugars is wide and there is an unrefined sugar type for all cooking, baking and general purpose uses. Unrefined sugars offer a natural source of colour and flavour, adding an extra dimension to both sweet and savoury cooking.

The Natural Unrefined Sugars

Golden Icing Sugar is made from unrefined cane sugar and has a natural golden colour – use for all types of icings and butter creams for topping and filling cakes and biscuits.

Golden Caster is a light, fine-grained, free-flowing sugar with a subtle 'buttery' taste and should be used in place of white caster sugar for all general baking.

Golden Granulated is the everyday, natural alternative to white sugar. Light coloured, and free-flowing, it is ideal for use in tea, on cereals and fresh fruits or for jams and brewing.

Organic Cane Sugar is free flowing and has a light golden colour. This sugar is a natural, organic general-purpose sugar for use in tea, coffee and home-baking.

Demerara, with its distinctive aroma and texture, is the traditional sugar for coffee. The large demerara crystals are ideal for topping cakes, biscuits and crumbles.

Sugar Crystals are the perfect sugar for coffee, dissolving slowly and releasing a beautiful enhancing rich flavour and aroma. The large, sparkling crystals also make a perfect crunchy topping for fruit cakes and biscuits.

Light Muscovado is the ultimate light soft brown sugar, with a warm honey colour and a glorious 'fudge like' flavour. It can be used to enrich both savoury and sweet recipes.

Dark Muscovado is the ultimate dark brown soft sugar, with a sticky texture, toffee flavour and rich aroma adding depth of flavour to savoury and sweet dishes.

Molasses sugar is the darkest sugar of all. This unique sugar contains the highest amount of natural molasses and gives extra flavour and moistness. Perfect for rich fruit cakes, mincemeat and also excellent for use in ethnic and barbecue cooking.

FRUIT CAKES

MY FAVOURITE FRUIT CAKE
My all time favourite fruit cake, which keeps well. It can be used as a special occasions cake, topped with marzipan and icing.

250 g (9 oz) margarine
250 g (9 oz) golden caster sugar
6 medium eggs
340 g (12 oz) plain flour and ...
5 ml (1 tsp) baking powder (sifted together)

170 g (6 oz) currants
170 g (6 oz) sultanas
140 g (5 oz) mixed chopped peel
140 g (5 oz) glacé cherries, halved

1. Cream margarine and sugar together until creamy and fluffy.
2. Add each of the eggs and beat well.
3. Gently fold in the flour and then stir in the fruit.
4. Spoon into a greased and lined 23 cm (9 ins) deep cake tin, and smooth the top.

5. **Baking:** 150°C, 300°F, Gas 2, and bake in the middle of the oven for $2^{1}/_{2}$–$3^{1}/_{4}$ hours, or in fan oven at 130°C for $2^{1}/_{4}$–$2^{1}/_{2}$ hours, until the skewer comes out clean and the cake is firm to touch and golden brown.

6. Leave to cool in the tin for 15 mins before turning onto a wire rack to cool completely.

APPLE AND WALNUT CAKE

A family friend gave me this recipe, a delightful use of apples.

225 g (8 oz) plain flour
5 ml (1 tsp) baking powder
10 ml (2 tsp) mixed spice
115 g (4 oz) butter
170 g (6 oz) dark muscovado sugar

3 medium eggs
115 g (4 oz) sultanas
115 g (4 oz) walnuts, chopped
225 g (8 oz) peeled eating apples, diced

1. Sift flour, baking powder and spice into a bowl.
2. Rub butter into flour until mixture resembles fine breadcrumbs.
3. Stir in remaining ingredients, mix well.
4. Grease and base line an 20.5 cm (8 ins) deep cake tin and place mixture in tin.

5. **Baking:** 170°C, 340°F, Gas 3, or fan oven 150°C, for $1^{1}/_4$–$1^{1}/_2$ hours. Cook until dark golden and springy to the touch. Leave to stand in tin for 30 mins before turning out.

PARADISE CAKE

340 g (12 oz) butter or margarine
225 g (8 oz) golden caster sugar
55 g (2 oz) set honey
5 medium eggs
225 (8 oz) plain flour, sieved
115 g (4 oz) self-raising flour, sieved
340 g (12 oz) sultanas

225 g (8 oz) glacé cherries, chopped
170 g (6 oz) glacé pineapple, chopped
85 g (3 oz) ready-to-eat apricots, chopped
55 g (2 oz) walnut pieces
55 g (2 oz) chopped mixed peel
finely grated zest and juice of 1 lemon
90–120 ml (6–8 tbsp) milk

1. Cream the margarine and sugar together until light and fluffy, then beat in the honey. Add each egg, beat well after each addition, adding a little flour to prevent any curdling.
2. Fold in the remaining flour, carefully stir in the prepared fruit, nuts and peel. Mix thoroughly then add the lemon zest and juice and enough milk to give a soft dropping consistency.
3. Lightly grease and line a 20.5 cm (8 ins) round deep cake tin. Place mixture in prepared tin and smooth over the top.

4. **Baking:** 160°C, 320°F, Gas 3, or fan oven 140°C, for $2^{1}/_2$–3 hours until the cake is firm to the touch and golden brown in colour. Allow to cool for 30 mins before turning out of tin.

APRICOT, PRUNE AND CHERRY CAKE

115 g (4 oz) ready-to-eat apricots
115 g (4 oz) ready-to-eat prunes
115 g (4 oz) glacé cherries
55 g (2 oz) dried cranberries
285 ml ($^1/_2$ pint) orange juice

170 g (6 oz) butter
170 g (6 oz) light muscovado sugar
225 g (8 oz) plain flour, sieved
2.5 ml ($^1/_2$ tsp) bicarbonate of soda
2 medium eggs

1. Chop the apricots, prunes and cherries, place in a large saucepan with the cranberries, orange juice, butter and sugar. Heat gently to melt the butter and dissolve the sugar. Bring to the boil and then simmer very gently for 15 mins, until mixture has thickened. Allow to cool for 15–20 mins.
2. Add the flour and bicarbonate of soda to the fruit mixture, then beat in the eggs and mix well.
3. Spoon mixture into a greased and lined 20.5 cm (8 ins) tin.

4. **Baking:** 170°C, 340°F, Gas 3, or fan oven 150°C, for $1^1/_4$–$1^1/_2$ hours until a skewer comes out clean. Allow to cool in tin.

GOLDEN CHRISTMAS CAKE
A light fruit cake ideal as an alternative to the traditional fruit cake.

115 g (4 oz) glacé pineapple
115 g (4 oz) glacé cherries
115 g (4 oz) walnuts
340 g (12 oz) sultanas
170 g (6 oz) butter

170 g (6 oz) light muscovado sugar
4 medium eggs
250 g (9 oz) self-raising flour, sieved
45 ml (3 tbsp) sherry

1. Chop the pineapple, cherries and walnuts, mix together with the sultanas.
2. Cream the butter and sugar together until light and creamy in colour. Add each egg and beat well, adding a little flour to avoid curdling.
3. Fold in the remaining flour with the fruit, nuts and sherry.
4. Lightly grease and line an 18 cm (7 ins) deep round cake tin, place prepared mixture in tin, smoothing the top, then hollowing out the centre.

5. **Baking:** 150°C, 300°F, Gas 2, or fan oven 130°C, for $2^1/_4$–$2^3/_4$ hours, until a skewer comes out clean and the cake is firm to the touch and golden brown. Leave to stand for 30 mins before turning out to cool completely.

6. **Icing:** This cake can be iced in the traditional way if so desired.

SEMI-RICH FRUIT CAKE
A light fruit cake ideal for lunch boxes

225 g (8 oz) plain flour and …
5 ml (1 tsp) baking powder, sifted together
115 g (4 oz) butter or margarine
115 g (4 oz) golden caster sugar

225 g (8 oz) mixed dried fruit
2 medium eggs, beaten
60 ml (4 tbsp) milk

1. Rub fat into flour until it resembles breadcrumbs.
2. Add the sugar, fruit, eggs and enough milk to give a soft dropping consistency.
3. Grease and line an 18 cm (7 ins) round cake tin. Turn into prepared tin.

4. **Baking:** 170°C, 340°F, Gas 3, or fan oven 150°C, for $1^1/4$–$1^1/2$ hours, until a skewer inserted in the centre comes out clean.

DUNDEE CAKE
A fairly rich Scottish fruit cake.

115 g (4 oz) raisins
115 g (4 oz) sultanas
115 g (4 oz) currants
55 g (2 oz) chopped mixed peel
grated zest of 1 lemon
170 g (6 oz) butter, softened
170 g (6 oz) golden caster sugar
3 medium eggs

225 g (8 oz) plain flour, sieved
pinch of salt
2.5 ml ($^1/2$ tsp) baking powder
2.5 ml ($^1/2$ tsp) mixed spice
15 ml (1 tbsp) sherry
55 g (2 oz) whole blanched almonds

1. Mix together the raisins, sultanas, currants, mixed peel and lemon zest.
2. In a mixing bowl cream together the butter and sugar until light and fluffy. Beat in the eggs, adding a spoon of flour if necessary to prevent the mixture from curdling.
3. Fold in the remaining flour, salt, baking powder and spice, mix well. Add the dried fruit and sherry and mix thoroughly.
4. Transfer the mixture to a greased and lined 18 cm (7 ins) round deep cake tin. Smooth the top and arrange the almonds on the top of the cake.

5. **Baking:** 160°C, 320°F, Gas 3, or fan oven 140°C, for $1^3/4$–$2^1/2$ hours or until a skewer inserted in the centre comes out clean. Remove from the tin and cool on a wire rack.

CHAIRMAN'S CAKE

This cake was designed for Mrs Eileen Meadmore for a celebration of her term of office as National Chairman following a request by two members of the National Executive Committee. "It's truly delicious! Quite the nicest fruit cake I've ever tasted. All those lovely big bits of nuts and fruit that I love munching into." (Eileen Meadmore)

115 g (4 oz) glacé cherries, halved
170 g (6 oz) ready-to-eat dried
   apricots, chopped
115 g (4 oz) ready-to-eat dried
   pineapple, chopped
115 g (4 oz) raisins
120 ml (8 tbsp) Drambuie
100 g (3¹/₂ oz) Brazil nuts
100 g (3¹/₂ oz) walnut halves

140 g (5 oz) butter
140 g (5 oz) dark muscovado sugar
225 g (8 oz) set honey
4 medium eggs
170 g (6 oz) plain flour
115 g (4 oz) ground almonds
200 g (7 oz) dark plain chocolate,
   cut into chunks

1. Place the prepared cherries, apricots, pineapple and raisins in a bowl, add the Drambuie, cover and leave to stand for 2–4 hours.
2. Roughly chop the nuts and add to the fruit mixture.
3. Cream the butter and sugar together in a large bowl until pale and fluffy. Stir in the honey, then beat in each egg. Fold in the flour and ground almonds, mixing well.
4. Carefully stir in the fruit, nuts and chocolate, blending evenly.
5. Spoon mixture into a greased and lined 23 cm (9 ins) deep round cake tin.

6. **Baking:** 140°C, 285°F, Gas 1, or fan oven 120°C, for 2–2¹/₂ hours or until a skewer inserted in the centre comes out clean. Remove from the oven and leave in the tin until cool. Cool completely on a wire rack.

7. Wrap the cold cake in foil and store for 5–7 days before serving.
8. Can be decorated with marzipan and icing for an extra special cake.

GOLDEN HARVEST CAKE

170 g (6 oz) margarine
115 g (4 oz) golden caster sugar
55 g (2 oz) honey
3 medium eggs
225 g (8 oz) brown self-raising flour. sieved

170 g (6 oz) sultanas
55 g (2 oz) walnuts, chopped
finely grated zest of 1 lemon
45–60 ml (3–4 tbsp) lemon juice

1. Cream the margarine and sugar together until light and fluffy, then beat in the honey. Add each egg, beating well after each addition, and adding a little flour to prevent any curdling.
2. Stir in the sultanas, walnuts and lemon zest, then fold in the remaining flour, adding enough lemon juice to give a soft dropping consistency.
3. Lightly grease and line an 18 cm (7 ins) deep cake tin. Place the mixture into the tin and smooth over the top.

4. **Baking:** 170°C, 340°F, Gas Mark 3, or fan oven 150°C, for $1^{1}/_{4}$–$1^{1}/_{2}$ hours, until firm to the touch and golden in colour. Allow to cool in the tin for 10 mins before turning onto cooling rack.

GUINNESS CAKE

A moist cake, which should be stored for at least a week before eating.

18 CM (7 INS) TIN	INGREDIENTS	20.5 CM (8 INS) TIN
170 g (6 oz)	raisins	225 g (8 oz)
170 g (6 oz)	sultanas	225 g (8 oz)
85 g (3 oz)	mixed peel, chopped	115 g (4 oz)
85 g (3 oz)	walnut pieces	115 g (4 oz)
90 ml (6 tbsp)	Guinness	120 ml (8 tbsp)
170 g (6 oz)	butter	225 g (8 oz)
170 g (6 oz)	light muscovado sugar	225 g (8 oz)
3	medium eggs	4
225 g (8 oz)	plain flour, sieved	285 g (10 oz)
5 ml (1 tsp)	mixed spice	7.5 ml ($1^{1}/_{2}$ tsp)

1. Place the raisins, sultanas, mixed peel and walnuts in a bowl, add the Guinness, cover and leave to soak for a minimum of 6 hours.
2. Cream the butter and sugar together until light and fluffy, gradually beat in the eggs, adding a little flour to stop mixture curdling.
3. Fold in the remaining flour and spice, then stir in the soaked fruit and any remaining liquid, mix well.
4. Grease and line the required deep round cake tin, spoon mixture into the prepared tin, smooth top and hollow centre slightly.

5. **Baking:** 150°C, 300°F, Gas 2, or fan oven 130°C, for $1^{3}/_{4}$–$2^{1}/_{2}$ hours until the cake is firm to the touch and until a skewer inserted in the centre comes out clean.

CHRISTMAS CAKE

A traditional recipe.

340 g (12 oz) raisins
340 g (12 oz) sultanas
340 g (12 oz) currants
55 g (2 oz) chopped mixed peel
115 g (4 oz) glacé cherries, chopped
grated rind and juice of 1 lemon
85 g (3 oz) flaked almonds

60 ml (4 tbsp) brandy
225 g (8 oz) butter
225 g (8 oz) dark muscovado sugar
4 medium eggs
250 g (9 oz) plain flour, sieved
5 ml (1 tsp) mixed spice
10 ml (2 tsp) black treacle

1. In a bowl mix together the raisins, sultanas, currants, mixed peel, cherries, rind and juice of 1 lemon and almonds, add the brandy, cover and leave for at least 6 hours.
2. In a mixing bowl cream butter and sugar until they become lighter in colour and fluffy. Beat in eggs, adding a little flour to prevent mixture from curdling.
3. Fold in the rest of the flour, spice, the soaked fruit and any remaining liquid and the treacle, mixing well.
4. Transfer the mixture to a greased and lined 20.5 cm (8 ins) deep round cake tin, level the top and slightly hollow the centre.

5. **Baking**: 150°C, 300°F, Gas 2, or fan oven 130°C, for 3–3$\frac{1}{2}$ hours or until a skewer inserted in the centre comes out clean. Leave in the tin for 15 mins before turning out onto a wire rack to cool completely. When cold, wrap in foil and store until required.

6. **Icing:** This cake can be iced in the traditional way, if so desired.

MODERN CHRISTMAS CAKE

Using a mixture of the new luxury dried fruit to make this traditional recipe.

200 g (7 oz) ready-to-eat apricots
170 g (6 oz) ready-to-eat figs
115 g (4 oz) ready-to-eat mango
115 g (4 oz) ready-to-eat pineapple
200 g (7 oz) glacé cherries
85 g (3 oz) sweetened dried blueberries
85 g (3 oz) sweetened dried cranberries
90 ml (6 tbsp) orange juice or brandy
250 g (9 oz) butter

250 g (9 oz) molasses sugar
4 medium eggs
115 g (4 oz) almonds, roughly chopped
grated zest of 1 orange
85 g (3 oz) ground almonds
225 g (8 oz) plain flour
10 ml (2 tsp) mixed spice
5 ml (1 tsp) cinnamon

1. Chop the apricots, figs, mango, pineapple and cherries coarsely, place into a large bowl with the blueberries and cranberries, stir in the orange juice or brandy, cover and leave to soak for at least 6 hours.
2. Beat together the butter and sugar until fluffy and lighter in colour. Beat in the eggs one at a time. Stir in the nuts and orange zest.
3. Sift together the flour and spices, add half to the creamed mixture with half the fruit, mix well. Add the remaining flour and fruit, mix thoroughly.
4. Place the mixture into a greased and lined 20.5 cm (8 ins) round deep cake tin and smooth the top.

5. **Baking:** 150°C, 300°F, Gas 2, or fan oven 120/130°C, for $2^{3/4}$–$3^{1/2}$ hours until the cake is firm to the touch and dark golden and a skewer inserted in the centre comes out clean.

6. Allow the cake to cool in the tin for 15 mins before turning out onto a wire rack to cool completely. Wrap the cake in foil and store in a dry, cool place until required.

SUNSHINE FRUIT CAKE
A moist fruit cake using tinned and dried fruit.

finely grated zest and juice of 1 lemon	225 g (8 oz) butter
200 g (7 oz) tin pineapple pieces	170 g (6 oz) golden caster sugar
225 g (8 oz) dried fruit salad	4 medium eggs
115 g (4 oz) sultanas	285 g (10 oz) self-raising flour, sieved
115 g (4 oz) raisins	
115 g (4 oz) mixed peel	

1. In a bowl place the lemon zest and juice, add the pineapple pieces and juice. Coarsely chop the dried fruit salad and add to the bowl with the sultanas, raisins and peel. Leave to soak for 1–2 hours.
2. In a large bowl cream the butter and sugar together until light and fluffy, beat in the eggs one at a time, adding a little flour to stop the mixture curdling.
3. Fold in remaining flour. Stir in the fruit and remaining juice, mixing well.
4. Spoon the mixture into a greased and lined 20.5 cm (8 ins) deep round cake tin and smooth the top, hollowing out the centre.

5. **Baking:** 170°C, 340°F, Gas 3, or fan oven 140/150°C, for $1^{3/4}$–$2^{1/4}$ hours until just firm to the touch and golden brown. Allow cake to cool in the tin for 15 mins before turning onto a rack to cool completely. Wrap in foil to store.

SIMNEL CAKE

A lightly spiced fruit cake, originally baked for Mothering Sunday by young girls in service, now more usually associated with Easter.

Marzipan:
225 g (8 oz) ground almonds
225 g (8 oz) golden caster sugar
115 g (4 oz) icing sugar
1 egg separated
juice of $^1/_2$ lemon

sieved apricot jam

Cake:
170 g (6 oz) butter or margarine
170 g (6 oz) light muscovado sugar
3 medium eggs
225 g (8 oz) plain flour
55 g (2 oz) glacé cherries, chopped
450 g (1 lb) mixed dried fruit
5 ml (1 tsp) mixed spice
2.5 ml ($^1/_2$ tsp) baking powder
grated zest of 1 lemon
30 ml (2 tbsp) milk
30 ml (2 tbsp) brandy

1. Make the marzipan. Mix almonds and sugar, add egg yolk and lemon juice. Mix to stiffish paste. Wrap marzipan in film and place in refrigerator.
2. Cream butter or margarine and sugar until light and fluffy.
3. Beat in eggs, adding tablespoon of measured flour with last egg.
4. Add fruit, spice, flour and baking powder, folding in to mix thoroughly.
5. Stir in lemon rind, milk and brandy.
6. Remove marzipan from refrigerator and divide in three pieces. Dust one piece with a little flour and roll into 18 cm (7 ins) round.
7. Line 18 cm (7 ins) cake tin with greased greaseproof paper. Place half cake mixture in prepared tin. Cover with marzipan and place remaining cake mixture on top. Smooth top.

8. **Baking:** 160°C, 320°F, Gas 3 for 2–2$^1/_4$ hours, or fan oven 140°C for 1$^3/_4$–2 hours, until cake springs back when pressed in centre and is golden brown:

9. Leave cake to stand in the tin for about 15 mins before turning out onto wire tray to cool.
10. When cold, remove the greaseproof paper and brush top of cake with apricot jam.
11. Roll out another piece of marzipan to fit top of cake and press in position.
12. Score top of marzipan to make diamond pattern and brush with egg white.
13. Roll the remaining marzipan into even-sized balls and press around the outer edge.
14. Place under the grill and toast gently until golden brown.

MAURITIAN EASTER CAKE

Serve with fromage frais as a special treat.

170 g (6 oz) self-raising flour
5 ml (1 tsp) baking powder
pinch of salt
115 g (4 oz) soft margarine
115 g (4 oz) light muscovado sugar
2 medium eggs
finely grated zest of 1 orange
10 ml (2 tsp) instant coffee blended with 30 ml (2 tbsp) orange juice
85 g (3 oz) raisins

Soaking syrup:
45 ml (3 tbsp) light muscovado sugar
30 ml (2 tbsp) orange juice
30 ml (2 tbsp) rum

1. Sift the flour, baking powder and salt into a bowl, add all the remaining ingredients, beat together with a wooden spoon for 2 mins until well blended.
2. Spoon into a greased and base-lined 900 g (2 lb) loaf tin.

3. **Baking:** 180°C, 355°F, Gas 4, or fan oven 160°C, for 50–65 mins until a skewer inserted into the centre comes out clean.

4. **To make the soaking syrup:** Place the sugar and orange juice into a saucepan, heat gently to dissolve the sugar, allow to cool, then stir in the rum. Pierce the warm cake several times across the top surface and drizzle the syrup over. Allow the cake to cool completely in the tin.

IRISH TEA BRACK

This is my brother's favourite cake which is his mother-in-law's recipe.

510 ml (18 fl oz) strong tea,
   made using 3 teabags
225 g (8 oz) dark muscovado sugar

510 g (1 lb 2 oz) mixed dried fruit
2 medium eggs
510 g (1 lb 2 oz) self-raising flour

1. Mix the tea and sugar together in a large mixing bowl, stir to dissolve the sugar. Add the fruit and leave to soak overnight.
2. Next day beat in the eggs, then carefully fold in the sieved flour.
3. Transfer the mixture into a 20.5 cm (8 ins) greased and lined deep cake tin.

4. **Baking:** 170°C, 340°F, Gas 3, or fan oven 150°C, for $1\frac{1}{2} - 2$ hours until well risen and a skewer inserted into the centre comes out clean. Leave in the tin for 10 mins before turning onto a wire rack to cool.

DATE AND WALNUT CAKE

85 g (3 oz) stoned dates
85 g (3 oz) walnuts
170 g (6 oz) margarine

170 g (6 oz) dark muscovado sugar
3 medium eggs
225 g (8 oz) self-raising flour, sieved

1. Chop the dates and walnuts roughly.
2. In a bowl cream the margarine and sugar together until pale and fluffy. Add the eggs one at a time beating well, stir in a little flour if mixture begins to curdle. Fold in the remaining flour and the prepared dates and walnuts.
3. Place the mixture into a greased and base-lined 900 g (2 lb) loaf tin, smooth the surface. The top can be sprinkled with granulated sugar.

4. **Baking:** 180°C, 355°F, Gas 4, or fan oven 160°C, for 60–75 mins until firm to touch and dark golden. Leave to cool in tin for 10 mins then turn onto rack.

HALF POUND CAKE

225 g (8 oz) butter or block margarine
115 g (4 oz) golden caster sugar
115 g (4 oz) light muscovado sugar
4 medium eggs, beaten
60 ml (4 tbsp) brandy
225 g (8 oz) raisins

225 g (8 oz) sultanas and currants mixed
170 g (6 oz) glacé cherries, chopped
225 g (8 oz) plain flour and ...
5 ml (1 tsp) mixed spice (sifted together)
walnut halves

1. Cream the butter and sugar together until pale and fluffy. Add the eggs, beating well after each addition, then stir in brandy.
2. Stir flour, fruit and cherries into the mixture gently.
3. Place mixture into a greased and lined 20.5 cm (8 ins) deep cake tin. Decorate top with walnut halves.

4. **Baking:** 150°C, 300°F, Gas 2, or fan oven 130°C, for 2–2$\frac{1}{2}$ hours

HIGHLAND FRUIT CAKE

225 g (8 oz) self-raising flour
pinch of salt
10 ml (2 tsp) mixed spice
115 g (4 oz) rolled oats
170 g (6 oz) sultanas

120 ml (8 tbsp) golden syrup
55 g (2 oz) golden caster sugar
225 g (8 oz) margarine
3 large eggs

1. Sift the flour, salt and spice into a bowl, then stir in the oats and sultanas.
2. Melt the syrup, sugar and margarine over a gentle heat.
3. Stir into dry ingredients, mixing well, then beat in the eggs.
4. Pour the mixture into a greased and lined 20.5 cm (8 ins) round cake tin.

5. **Baking:** 180°C, 355°F, Gas 4, or fan oven 160°C, for 1–1½ hours or until a skewer inserted in the centre comes out clean. Leave in tin for 15 mins. Turn onto rack.

MARMALADE AND COURGETTE CAKE

170 g (6 oz) mixed dried fruit
finely grated zest and juice of 1 lemon
225 g (8 oz) courgette, grated
115 g (4 oz) lemon marmalade

115 g (4 oz) margarine
115 g (4 oz) demerara sugar
2 medium eggs
225 g (8 oz) wholemeal self-raising flour

1. Place the dried fruit, lemon zest and juice in a bowl and leave for about 30 mins. Stir in the grated courgette and marmalade.
2. In a bowl cream the margarine and sugar together until light in colour, then beat in the eggs. Stir in the flour, add the fruit mixture, mix well.
3. Place the mixture into a greased and lined 20.5 cm (8 ins) deep round cake tin.

4. **Baking:** 160°C, 320°F, Gas 3, or fan oven 140°C, for 50–60 mins until cake springs back when pressed in the centre. Leave to cool in the tin.

BOILED FRUIT CAKE

140 g (5 oz) butter
170 g (6 oz) golden syrup
170 ml (6 fl oz) milk
450 g (1 lb) mixed fruit
55 g (2 oz) chopped cherries
115 g (4 oz) walnuts, chopped

225 g (8 oz) plain flour, sieved
2.5 ml (½ tsp) bicarbonate of soda
10 ml (2 tsp) mixed spice
2 medium eggs
30 ml (2 tbsp) brandy

1. Place butter, syrup, milk, fruit, cherries and nuts into a saucepan, heat to melt together, simmer for 5 mins, then allow to cool for 30 mins.
2. Stir in remaining ingredients and mix together well. Place in a greased and lined 20.5 cm (8 ins) deep cake tin.

3. **Baking:** 150°C, 300°F, Gas 2, or fan oven 130°C, for 1½–2 hours Leave to cool in tin for 15 mins before turning out and cooling.

LARGE CAKES

BANANA BUTTERSCOTCH CAKE

115 g (4 oz) self-raising flour
115 g (4 oz) wholemeal self-raising flour
115 g (4 oz) butter
115 g (4 oz) dark muscovado sugar
2 medium eggs
450 g (1 lb) ripe bananas, weighed in their skins

Frosting:
130 g (4¼ oz) low fat cream cheese
finely grated zest of 1 lemon
15 ml (1 tbsp) dark muscovado sugar
banana chips to decorate

1. Sieve the flours into a bowl and rub in the butter, until the mixture resembles breadcrumbs. Stir in the sugar. Beat in the eggs.
2. Peel and mash the bananas and fold into the mixture to give a soft dropping consistency.
3. Place mixture into a greased and lined 18 cm (7 ins) deep round cake tin.

4. **Baking:** 180°C, 355°F, Gas 4, or fan oven 160°C, for 50–65 mins or until a skewer inserted in the centre comes out clean. Allow to cool in the tin for 10 mins before turning onto a rack to cool completely.

5. **To make the frosting:** Mix together the cream cheese, lemon zest and sugar. When the cake is cold, split the cake horizontally and spread the frosting in the centre, sides and top.

CHERRY CAKE

225 g (8 oz) butter, softened
225 g (8 oz) golden caster sugar
4 medium eggs, whisked lightly
225 g (8 oz) plain flour
2.5 ml ($\frac{1}{2}$ tsp) baking powder

250 g (9 oz) glacé cherries, quartered
115 g (4 oz) ground almonds
a few drops almond essence
15 ml (1 tbsp) milk
30 ml (2 tbsp) demerara sugar

1. Cream the butter and sugar together until light, pale and fluffy.
2. Beat in the whisked egg a little at a time. Sift the flour and baking powder together and carefully fold this into the creamed mixture using a metal spoon.
3. Carefully fold in the cherries and ground almonds into the cake, adding one or two drops of almond essence and the milk.
4. Grease and line a 20.5 cm (8 ins) deep cake tin. Spoon the cake mix into the prepared tin, level off the top with the back of a spoon, then sprinkle with the demerara sugar.

5. **Baking:** 180°C, 355°F, Gas 4, or fan oven 160°C for $1\frac{1}{4}$–$1\frac{1}{2}$ hours, until the cake has shrunk away from the side of the tin and the centre is springy to touch.

6. Cool the cake in the tin for 15 mins before turning it out on to a wire rack to cool. Store in a tin.

VARIATION:
Use 85 g (3 oz) desiccated coconut in place of 85 g (3 oz) glacé cherries; it may be necessary to add an extra drop of milk.

CHERRY AND ALMOND CAKE

115 g (4 oz) butter
115 g (4 oz) margarine
225 g (8 oz) golden caster sugar
3 medium eggs
1.25 ml ($^1/_4$ tsp) almond essence

225 g (8 oz) plain flour
5 ml (1 tsp) baking powder
115 g (4 oz) ground almond
115 g (4 oz) glacé cherries
golden granulated sugar for sprinkling

1. Cream the butter, margarine and sugar together until light and fluffy. Gradually beat in the eggs and almond essence.
2. Sieve the flour, baking powder and ground almonds and fold into mixture, gently stir in the chopped cherries.
3. Grease and line a 20.5 cm (8 ins) deep round cake tin. Place the prepared mixture in the tin, smooth the top and then sprinkle with the granulated sugar.

4. **Baking:** 140°C, 285°F, Gas 1, or fan oven 120°C, for $1^3/_4$–$2^1/_4$ hours until the cake is firm to the touch and golden brown. Cool for 15 mins in the tin before turning out to cool completely.

OLD FASHIONED SEED CAKE
Can be served plain or buttered.

285 g (10 oz) self-raising flour
140 g (5 oz) butter
140 g (5 oz) light muscovado sugar
30 g (1 oz) caraway seeds
55 g (2 oz) chopped mixed peel

finely grated zest and juice of 1 lemon
2.5 ml ($^1/_2$ tsp) mixed spice
2 medium eggs
75–90 ml (5–6 tbsp) milk
demerara sugar

1. Sift the flour into a bowl and rub in the butter until the mixture resembles fine breadcrumbs.
2. Stir in the sugar, caraway seeds, mixed peel, lemon zest and mixed spice.
3. Beat the eggs, then stir into the dry ingredients with the lemon juice and enough milk to form a soft dropping consistency.
4. Turn the mixture into a greased and lined 18 cm (7 ins) round cake tin.

5. **Baking:** 180°C, 355°F, Gas 4, or fan oven 160°C, for 1–$1^1/_4$ hours until the cake is well risen and springy to the touch. Allow to cool in the tin for 10 mins before turning onto a rack to cool. Sprinkle top with demerara sugar before serving.

COFFEE AND ALMOND CAKE

A lightly flavoured cake which improves with storage.

115 g (4 oz) butter or margarine
115 g (4 oz) golden caster sugar
2 medium eggs
30 ml (2 tbsp) coffee essence

45 ml (3 tbsp) sherry
140 g (5 oz) self-raising flour, sieved
55 g (2 oz) ground almonds
15 g ($^1/_2$ oz) chopped almonds

1. Cream the butter and sugar together until light and fluffy, then beat in each egg, coffee essence, 1 tbsp sherry and a little sieved flour.
2. Carefully fold in the remaining flour and ground almonds.
3. Lightly grease and line a 15 cm (6 ins) deep cake tin, place mixture in tin and smooth top. Sprinkle chopped almonds over the top.

4. **Baking:** 160°C, 320°F, Gas 3, or fan oven 140°C, for 1–1$^1/_2$ hours until firm to the touch and golden brown. Leave to cool in tin for 10 mins before turning out to cool completely.

5. Prick base and pour remaining sherry over, wrap tightly in foil and leave for 3–4 days before eating.

LEMON AND CARDAMOM CAKE

Traditional flavours give this cake a twist.

170 g (6 oz) margarine
170 g (6 oz) golden caster sugar
3 medium eggs

170 g (6 oz) self-raising flour, sieved
finely grated zest and juice of 1 lemon
6 cardamom pods, seeds removed and
    crushed

1. Cream the margarine and sugar together until light and fluffy. Gradually add the eggs, beating well.
2. Fold in the flour, stir in the lemon zest, juice and crushed cardamom seeds, mix well.
3. Spoon mixture into a greased and based lined 28 x 18 cm (11 x 7 ins) tin.

4. **Baking:** 180°C, 355°F, Gas 4, or fan oven 160°C, for 35–45 mins until golden and springy to the touch. Allow to cool in the tin.

5. For a change, top with a lemon icing, see LEMON AND GINGER CAKE (p. 30).
6. Cut into squares to serve.

LEMON AND GINGER CAKE

285 g (10 oz) plain flour
5 ml (1 tsp) bicarbonate of soda
10 ml (2 tsp) ground ginger
115 g (4 oz) soft margarine
115 g (4 oz) light muscovado sugar
30 g (1 oz) stem ginger, finely chopped
1 medium egg
200 ml (7 fl oz) milk
250 g (9 oz) golden syrup

Icing:
finely grated zest and juice
    of 1 small lemon
170 g (6 oz) golden icing sugar
85 g (3 oz) soft margarine

To finish:
30 g (1 oz) flaked almonds

1. Sift the plain flour, bicarbonate of soda and ginger into a bowl. Add the remaining ingredients and mix to a thick smooth batter.
2. Pour the mixture into a 25.5 x 20.5 cm (10 x 8 ins) greased and base-lined tin and smooth the top.

3. **Baking:** 150°C, 300°F, Gas 2, or fan oven 130°C, for 1–1½ hours until set and golden. A skewer inserted in the centre should come out clean. Leave in the tin for 10 mins before cooling on a wire rack.

4. **To make the icing:** Place the zest and juice of the lemon in a bowl, add the sieved icing sugar and the margarine and beat until smooth. Spread the icing over the top and sides of the cake and sprinkle with the flaked almonds.

COCONUT CAKE

170 g (6 oz) self-raising flour
2.5 ml (½ tsp) baking powder
170 g (6 oz) soft margarine

85 g (3 oz) desiccated coconut
170 g (6 oz) golden caster sugar
3 medium eggs

1. Sieve the flour and baking powder into a bowl, add the remaining ingredients. Beat with a wooden spoon for 2–3 mins until blended.
2. Spoon the mixture into greased and lined 18 cm (7 ins) round cake tin.

3. **Baking:** 180°C, 355°F, Gas 4, or fan oven 160°C, for 1–1½ hours until well risen and golden. A skewer inserted in the centre should come out clean. Leave in the tin for 5 mins before turning out onto a rack to cool completely.

LEMON DRIZZLE CAKE

170 g (6 oz) margarine
170 g (6 oz) golden caster sugar
2 medium eggs
60 ml (4 tbsp) milk

170 g (6 oz) self-raising flour
grated zest and juice of 1 lemon
15 ml (1 tbsp) icing sugar

1. Cream the margarine and sugar together until light and fluffy, gradually beat in the eggs and milk.
2. Sieve the flour and fold into mixture with the grated lemon zest.
3. Grease and base line a 900 g (2 lb) loaf tin, place prepared mixture in tin.

4. **Baking:** 180°C, 355°F, Gas 4, or fan oven 160°C, for 50–65 mins until cake is golden brown and firm to the touch.

5. Mix the lemon juice and icing sugar together and pour over the cake as soon as it is removed from the oven.
6. Allow the glaze to set before removing the cake from the tin.

RICH ALMOND CAKE

115 g (4 oz) butter
140 g (5 oz) golden caster sugar
3 medium eggs
85 g (3 oz) ground almonds

45 g ($1\frac{1}{2}$ oz) plain flour, sieved
2–3 drops almond essence

extra sugar for dredging

1. Cream the butter until soft, add sugar and beat until light and fluffy. Add the eggs one at a time and beat well, add one third of the almonds with each egg.
2. Fold in flour and almond essence.
3. Lightly grease and base line a deep 18 cm (7 ins) sandwich cake tin, place mixture into tin, smooth top.

4. **Baking:** 180°C, 355°F, Gas 4, or fan oven 160°C, for 30–45 mins until firm to the touch, golden in colour, and beginning to shrink away from the sides of the tin.

5. Leave to cool for 5 mins before turning out onto a cooling rack to cool completely.
6. Dredge with a little sugar before serving.

PASSION CAKE

225 g (8 oz) butter
225 g (8 oz) light muscovado sugar
4 medium eggs, separated
finely grated zest and juice of 1 lemon
170 g (6 oz) wholemeal self-raising flour
5 ml (1 tsp) baking powder
55 g (2 oz) ground almonds
115 g (4 oz) walnuts chopped
340 g (12 oz) carrots, peeled and grated

Topping:
55 g (2 oz) butter, softened
225 g (8 oz) golden icing sugar
115 g (4 oz) low fat cream cheese
45 ml (3 tbsp) lemon curd
5 ml (1 tsp) lemon juice
55 g (2 oz) walnut halves

1. Cream the butter and sugar together in a bowl until pale and fluffy. Beat in the egg yolks, then stir in the lemon zest and juice.
2. Sieve the flour and baking powder together, fold into creamed mixture, stir in the almonds and walnuts.
3. In a clean grease-free bowl whisk the egg whites until stiff, fold into the cake mixture with the carrots, mixing thoroughly.
4. Grease and line a 20.5 cm (8 ins) deep round cake tin. Put mixture into tin, smooth the top and hollow the centre slightly.

5. **Baking:** 180°C, 355°F, Gas 4, or fan oven 160°C, for $1^{1}/_{4}$–$1^{3}/_{4}$ hours until firm to the touch and golden. Leave to cool slightly in the tin, then turn onto a rack to cool completely.

6. **To make the icing:** Place all the icing ingredients, except the walnut halves, in a bowl and beat together until smooth.

7. Cut cake in half, spread icing on one half, sandwich together and spread the remaining icing over top and sides of cake. Decorate top with walnut halves.

SIMPLE GINGER CAKE
Softly flavoured, using ginger marmalade.

170 g (6 oz) margarine
170 g (6 oz) light muscovado sugar
3 medium eggs
115 g (4 oz) ginger marmalade
225 g (8 oz) self-raising flour, sieved
5 ml (1 tsp) ground ginger

Icing:
55 g (2 oz) ginger marmalade
85 g (3 oz) golden icing sugar

1. In a bowl beat the margarine and sugar together until pale in colour and fluffy. Add the eggs, beating well, stir in a little flour to stop mixture curdling.
2. Stir in the marmalade, the remaining flour and ginger, blend evenly.
3. Turn the mixture into a greased and lined 18 cm (7 ins) round cake tin.

4. **Baking:** 170°C, 340°F, Gas 3, or fan oven 150°C, for $1^{1}/_4$–$1^{1}/_2$ hours until firm to the touch and golden. Turn onto a rack to cool.

5. **To make the icing:** Place the marmalade in a small bowl and stir in the sieved icing sugar. Spread evenly over the top of the cake.

6. Place cake under a hot grill to dissolve the sugar into the cake. Remember to take care so it does not burn. Allow to cool and set before serving.

    VARIATION: Try different flavoured marmalades.

SANDCAKE

This cake is based on a Danish traditional cake, similar to a Madeira cake.

170 g (6 oz) butter, softened
170 g (6 oz) golden caster sugar
3 medium eggs
115 g (4 oz) plain flour, sifted
5 ml (1 tsp) baking powder, sifted

115 g (4 oz) cornflour, sifted
2.5 ml ($^{1}/_2$ tsp) almond essence
30 ml (2 tbsp) milk to mix
30 g (1 oz) flaked almonds
icing sugar to finish

1. Cream the butter and caster sugar until light and fluffy, then beat in the eggs one at a time.
2. Gradually fold in the sieved flour, baking powder and cornflour.
3. Add the almond essence and milk to give a soft dropping consistency.
4. Line the length and ends of a 900 g (2 lb) loaf tin with lightly greased greaseproof paper. Place the mixture in the tin and level the surface. Sprinkle on the flaked almonds.

5. **Baking:** 180°C, 355°F, Gas 4, or fan oven 160°C, for 1–$1^{1}/_2$ hours, until golden brown and firm to touch.

6. Leave to cool in tin for 10 mins before lifting out of tin and allowing to cool completely. Sprinkle generously with sieved icing sugar.

    VARIATION: Make a lemon glacé icing to coat the top and sides.

RUM AND ORANGE CAKE

finely grated zest and juice of 2 oranges
45 ml (3 tbsp) rum
170 g (6 oz) margarine

170 g (6 oz) golden caster sugar
3 medium eggs
225 g (8 oz) plain flour, sieved
7.5 ml (1½ tsp) baking powder, sieved

1. Place orange zest and juice in a small basin with the rum, leave overnight.
2. Cream the margarine and sugar together until light and fluffy.
3. Separate the eggs, placing the whites in a large clean bowl.
4. Add the egg yolks to the creamed mixture, beating well. Stir in the flour, baking powder and the orange and rum mixture, mix well.
5. Whisk egg whites until they form soft peaks, then lightly fold into the mixture.
6. Grease and line an 18 cm (7 ins) deep round cake tin. Place mixture in tin and smooth the top.

7. **Baking:** 170°C, 340°F, Gas 3, or fan oven 150°C, for 1¼–1½ hours, until firm to touch and golden colour. Leave to cool in tin for 10 mins, turn onto cooling rack.

SPICED HONEY CAKE

A spicy honey cake with ginger pieces.

170 g (6 oz) butter
85 g (3 oz) golden caster sugar
85 g (3 oz) clear honey
3 medium eggs, separated
225 g (8 oz) self-raising flour
5 ml (1 tsp) ground cinnamon

5 ml (1 tsp) ground ginger
30 g (1 oz) stem ginger, chopped
10 ml (2 tsp) ginger syrup
grated zest and juice of 1 orange

icing sugar for dredging

1. Cream together butter, sugar and honey until light and fluffy. Beat in egg yolks.
2. Sieve the flour and spices, stir into the creamed mixture with the ginger pieces, syrup, orange zest and juice, mix well.
3. In a clean bowl whisk the egg whites until stiff. Fold into the mixture.
4. Place into a greased and base-lined 20.5 cm (8 ins) deep round cake tin.

5. **Baking:** 180°C, 355°F, Gas 4, or fan oven 160°C, for 50–70 mins until well risen, firm to the touch and golden brown in colour.

6. Allow to cool slightly before turning out and dredging with icing sugar whilst still warm.

SNOW WHITE CAKE

225 g (8 oz) shortcrust pastry
340 g (12 oz) glacé cherries
55 g (2 oz) soft margarine
55 g (2 oz) golden caster sugar
1 large egg
10 ml (2 tsp) coffee essence
55 g (2 oz) self-raising flour
30 g (1 oz) walnuts, chopped
little milk

Topping:
85 g (3 oz) butter, softened
60 ml (4 tbsp) double cream
45 g (1½ oz) cocoa powder, sieved
85 g (3 oz) bitter chocolate

1. **Make pastry,** using 225 g (8 oz) plain flour, 55 g (2 oz) hard margarine and 55 g (2 oz) lard. Rub fat into flour until mixture resembles breadcrumbs, add enough water to mix, knead gently.
2. Roll out the pastry on a lightly flowered surface to a circle large enough to line the base and sides of a 23 cm (9 ins) flan dish. Prick the bottom of the pastry well with a fork.
3. Drain the cherries and put aside.
4. Beat together the margarine, sugar, egg and coffee essence. Stir in gently the sieved flour and then the chopped walnuts. Add a very little milk to give the mixture a soft consistency.
5. Pour half the mixture into the pastry-lined tin. Sprinkle the drained cherries on top and then spoon on the remainder of the sponge mixture.

6. **Baking:** 170°C, 340°F, Gas 3, or fan oven 150°C, for 35–45 mins, or until well risen and springy to the touch. Leave to cool in the tin, then transfer to a serving plate.

7. **To make the topping**: Beat 55 g (2 oz) butter with the cream and sieved cocoa powder. Melt the chocolate with the rest of the butter and cool slightly. Carefully stir in the cream mixture.
8. Cool, then spread over the top of the cake, swirling with the back of a spoon. Leave topping to set before serving the cake. Cut into wedges.

PARKIN

225 g (8 oz) plain flour
10 ml (2 tsp) baking powder
15 ml (1 tbsp) ground ginger
115 g (4 oz) margarine
225 g (8 oz) medium oatmeal

115 g (4 oz) golden caster sugar
170 g (6 oz) golden syrup
170 g (6 oz) black treacle
60 ml (4 tbsp) milk
1 medium egg

1. In a mixing bowl sift together the flour, baking powder and ginger. Rub in the margarine until the mixture resembles breadcrumbs, then stir in oatmeal and sugar.
2. In a saucepan gently melt the golden syrup and treacle.
3. Make a well in the centre of the dry ingredients and pour in the syrup, treacle, milk and egg. Mix to a smooth thick batter.
4. Pour mixture into greased and base-lined 25.5 x 20.5 x 4 cm (10 x 8 x 1½ ins) tin.

5. **Baking:** 180°C, 355°F, Gas 4, or fan oven 160°C, for 45–60 mins until the mixture springs back when lightly pressed and has started to shrink away from the sides of the tin.

6. Turn out and cool on a wire rack. Wrap in foil to store.

STICKY GINGERBREAD

A lovely sticky cake that keeps well.

225 g (8 oz) butter or margarine
225 g (8 oz) dark muscovado sugar
225 g (8 oz) black treacle
340 g (12 oz) plain flour
2 medium eggs, beaten

15 ml (1 tbsp) ground ginger
10 ml (2 tsp) ground cinnamon
pinch of salt
5 ml (1 tsp) bicarbonate of soda
285 ml (½ pint) warm milk

1. Melt together slowly the treacle, sugar and butter, stirring all the time.
2. Remove from heat and stir in beaten eggs.
3. Sieve flour, salt, cinnamon and ginger. Stir in melted mixture.
4. Sieve bicarbonate of soda into a bowl. Add warm milk.
5. Add treacle mixture. Stir into mixture and mix well.
6. Line 25.5 cm (10 in) square tin with greased greaseproof paper. Pour mixture into tin.

7. **Baking:** 140°C, 285°F, Gas 1, or fan oven 120°C, for 1–1½ hours.

It may be necessary to cover surface of cake with greaseproof paper after one hour to prevent overbaking.

8. Allow gingerbread to cool before removing from tin and greaseproof paper.
9. Cut into thick slices and spread with butter.
10. Store in airtight tin or wrapped in foil. This cake keeps well.

ST CLEMENT'S CAKE
A tangy blend of lemon and orange flavours.

170 g (6 oz) margarine
115 g (4 oz) golden granulated sugar
3 medium eggs

200 g (7 oz) self-raising flour, sieved
170 g (6 oz) orange marmalade
grated zest and juice of 1 lemon

1. Beat the margarine and sugar together in a bowl until light and fluffy. Beat in the eggs, gradually, adding flour if mixture looks like it is curdling.
2. Fold in remaining flour. Stir in marmalade, lemon zest and juice, mixing well.
3. Spoon mixture into a greased and base-lined 28 x 18 cm (11 x 7 ins) tin.

4. **Baking:** 180°C, 355°F, Gas 4, or fan oven 160°C, for 35–45 mins until golden and springy to touch. Allow to cool in the tin. Cut into squares to serve.

PEACH AND ALMOND CAKE

170 g (6 oz) self-raising flour, sieved
2.5 ml (¹/₂ tsp) baking powder, sieved
170 g (6 oz) butter, softened
170 g (6 oz) golden caster sugar
30 ml (2 tbsp) Amaretto liqueur
3 medium eggs

2 large peaches, peeled, stoned and diced
115 g (4 oz) ground almonds

Topping:
30 g (1 oz) flaked almonds
30 ml (2 tbsp) demerara sugar

1. Place the flour, baking powder, butter, sugar, eggs and liqueur into a bowl and beat well until well blended.
2. Toss chopped peaches in the ground almonds to coat. Stir into cake mixture.
3. Grease and base line a 20.5 cm (8 ins) square tin, place mixture in tin.
4. Mix together flaked almonds and sugar, sprinkle over top of mixture.

5. **Baking:** 180°C, 355°F, Gas 4, or fan oven 160°C, for 45–60 mins until springy to the touch and golden.

TEA LOAVES

APPLE TEA BREAD

A tea bread that is moist and fruity and keeps well.

340 g (12 oz) cooking apples,
    peeled, cored and diced
5 ml (1 tsp) mixed spice
45 ml (3 tbsp) honey
115 g (4 oz) butter, softened
115 g (4 oz) demerara sugar

2 medium eggs
250 g (9 oz) self raising flour, sifted
55 g (2 oz) ground almonds
1 red eating apple, cored and sliced
15 ml (1 tbsp) honey

1. Place prepared cooking apples in a saucepan with spice and honey, simmer gently for 10 mins.
2. Cream together the butter and sugar, add eggs, beating well. Fold in flour and almonds, mix the stewed apples in carefully.
3. Line the base and lightly grease a 900 g (2 lb) loaf tin. Spoon mixture into tin and level the top. Arrange apple slices over top of mixture.

4. **Baking:** 180°C, 355°F, Gas 4, or fan oven 160°C, for 50–60 mins, until firm to touch and dark golden.

5. Remove the loaf from the oven and brush honey over it. Allow to cool before removing from tin. Can be served plain or buttered.

   VARIATION: Replace ground almonds with ground hazelnuts.

BANANA TEA LOAF

85 g (3 oz) glacé cherries
55 g (2 oz) walnuts
450 g (1 lb) ripe bananas
  (weighed in their skins)
225 g (8 oz) self-raising flour
2.5 ml ($\frac{1}{2}$ tsp) baking powder

170 g (6 oz) light muscovado sugar
115 g (4 oz) sultanas
55 g (2 oz) chopped mixed peel
2 medium eggs
115 g (4 oz) soft margarine

1. Chop the cherries and walnuts. Mash the bananas.
2. Sieve the flour and baking powder into a mixing bowl, add the prepared cherries, walnuts and bananas, then stir in the remaining ingredients. Mix well and beat for one minute with a wooden spoon.
3. Place the mixture in a greased and base-lined 900 g (2 lb) loaf tin and smooth the top.

4. **Baking:** 170°C, 340°F, Gas 3, or fan oven 150°C, for $1\frac{1}{4}$–$1\frac{3}{4}$ hours until well risen, golden and firm to touch. Leave in tin for 5 mins before cooling.

Note: This loaf keeps well wrapped in foil. It can be served plain or buttered.

CRANBERRY AND APRICOT TEA BREAD

395 g (14 oz) plain flour
2.5 ml ($\frac{1}{2}$ tsp) salt
7.5 ml ($1\frac{1}{2}$ tsp) baking powder
2.5 ml ($\frac{1}{2}$ tsp) bicarbonate of soda
170 g (6 oz) golden caster sugar
115 g (4 oz) ready-to-eat dried cranberries
170 g (6 oz) ready-to-eat dried apricots, cut into pieces

30 g (1 oz) butter, melted
1 medium egg, beaten
grated rind of 1 lemon
285 ml ($\frac{1}{2}$ pint) orange juice

1. Sift flour, salt, baking powder and bicarbonate into a large bowl. Add sugar, cranberries and apricots. Mix well. Add remaining ingredients. Mix thoroughly.
2. Place mixture into a greased and base-lined 900 g (2 lb) loaf tin.

3. **Baking:** 180°C, 355°F, Gas 4, or fan oven 160°C, for 50–60 mins, until golden brown.

4. When cooked, leave to cool, then store in an airtight container.

DATE AND CHERRY TEA LOAF

115 g (4 oz) soft margarine
45 ml (3 tbsp) golden syrup
45 ml (3 tbsp) black treacle
140 ml ($^1/_4$ pint) milk
1 medium egg
115 g (4 oz) dates
55 g (2 oz) glacé cherries

55 g (2 oz) walnuts
340 g (12 oz) plain flour
5 ml (1 tsp) baking powder
2.5 ml ($^1/_2$ tsp) bicarbonate of soda

icing sugar to dredge

1. Place the margarine, syrup, treacle, milk and egg into a mixing bowl. Roughly chop the cherries, dates and walnuts and add to the syrup mixture.
2. Sieve the flour, baking powder and bicarbonate of soda into the mixture and beat together with a wooden spoon for 2–3 mins until blended.
3. Spoon mixture into greased and base-lined 900 g (2 lb) loaf tin, smooth the top.

4. **Baking:** 170°C, 340°F, Gas 3, or fan oven 150°C, for 1$^1/_4$–1$^3/_4$ hours until well risen and golden. Turn onto a wire rack to cool.

5. When cold, sprinkle thickly with icing sugar and melt under a hot grill.

DATE AND WALNUT TEA BREAD

285 ml ($^1/_2$ pint) milk
85 g (3 oz) black treacle
55 g (2 oz) butter
340 g (12 oz) plain flour
15 ml (1 tbsp) baking powder

2.5 ml ($^1/_2$ tsp) bicarbonate of soda
2.5 ml ($^1/_2$ tsp) salt
85 g (3 oz) light muscovado sugar
115 g (4 oz) dates
115 g (4 oz) walnuts

1. In a saucepan warm the milk, treacle and butter together until just melted.
2. Sift the flour, baking powder and salt into a bowl and stir in the sugar.
3. Coarsely chop the dates and walnuts, stir into the dry ingredients, add the liquid and mix thoroughly to form a smooth thick batter.
4. Pour the mixture into a 900 g (2 lb) greased and lined loaf tin.

5. **Baking:** 170°C, 340°F, Gas 3, or fan oven 150°C, for 1–1$^1/_4$ hours until well risen, set, and a skewer inserted in the centre comes out clean. Leave to stand in the tin for 10 mins before turning onto a wire rack to cool completely.

6. Serve plain or buttered.

SPICED PLUM TEA BREAD

115 g (4 oz) ready-to-eat prunes
115 g (4 oz) raisins
115 g (4 oz) sultanas
30 ml (2 tbsp) brandy
225 g (8 oz) wholemeal self-raising flour
5 ml (1 tsp) baking powder
5 ml (1 tsp) cinnamon
5 ml (1 tsp) mixed spice
2.5 ml ($\frac{1}{2}$ tsp) salt
170 g (6 oz) soft margarine
170 g (6 oz) light muscovado sugar
3 medium eggs

1. Chop the prunes roughly, place in a bowl with the raisins, sultanas and brandy, leave to soak for 30 mins.
2. Sieve into a mixing bowl the flour, baking powder, spices and salt. Stir in the margarine, sugar, eggs and the fruit. Beat well for 1 minute with a wooden spoon.
3. Place mixture into a greased and base-lined 900 g (2 lb) loaf tin. Smooth the top.

4. **Baking:** 140°C, 285°F, Gas 1, or fan oven 120°C, for 2–2$\frac{1}{2}$ hours until well risen and when a skewer inserted in the centre comes out clean.

5. Turn out and cool on a rack.

PINEAPPLE COCONUT TEA LOAF

A moist tea loaf which slices well, ideal for lunch boxes.

395 g (14 oz) can pineapple pieces
115 g (4 oz) butter, softened
115 g (4 oz) light muscovado sugar
2 medium eggs
140 g (5 oz) wholemeal flour
10 ml (2 tsp) baking powder
5 ml (1 tsp) cinnamon
85 g (3 oz) desiccated coconut

1. Drain the pineapple pieces well.
2. Place all the ingredients into a bowl and beat together with a wooden spoon for 3 minutes, or with a hand mixer for 1 minute, until well mixed.
3. Grease and line a 900 g (2 lb) loaf tin, spoon mixture into tin and smooth the top.
4. **Baking:** 180°C, 355°F, or fan oven 160°C, for 1–1$\frac{1}{2}$ hours, until skewer inserted in the cake comes out clean.

5. Leave to cool in the tin for 10 mins before turning out onto a wire rack to cool completely.

TROPICAL FRUIT TEA LOAF

Makes 2 x 450 g (1 lb) loaves. Using a fruit cordial makes an interesting tea loaf. You could use fruit teabags instead.

55 ml (2 fl oz) fruit cordial made up to –
425 ml (³/₄ pint) with hot water
115 g (4 oz) ready-to-eat prunes
115 g (4 oz) ready-to-eat pears
115 g (4 oz) ready-to-eat pineapple
115 g (4 oz) ready-to-eat peaches
115 g (4 oz) ready-to-eat papaya

225 g (8 oz) ready-to-eat apricots
115 g (4 oz) walnuts
225 g (8 oz) light muscovado sugar
2 medium eggs
225 g (8 oz) wholemeal self-raising
   flour, sieved together with …
225 g (8 oz) self-raising flour

1. Chop fruit into evenly sized pieces. Soak for about 1 hour in the hot cordial.
2. Stir in the walnuts, sugar, eggs and flour, mix together thoroughly.
3. Grease and line two 450 g (1 lb) loaf tins and divide the mixture evenly between the tins.

4. **Baking:** 170°C, 340°F, Gas 3, or fan oven 150°C, until well risen and firm to the touch.

5. Leave to cool in the tin for 10 mins before placing on a cooling rack to cool completely.

MIXED FRUIT TEA LOAF

115 g (4 oz) golden syrup
55 g (2 oz) black treacle
55 g (2 oz) butter
115 g (4 oz) golden caster sugar
285 g (10 oz) brown self-raising flour

5 ml (1 tsp) mixed spice
225 g (8 oz) dried mixed fruit
2 medium eggs
60 ml (4 tbsp) milk

1. In a saucepan measure the syrup and treacle, add the butter and sugar and gently heat until all ingredients have melted. Remove from the heat.
2. Sieve the flour and spice into a mixing bowl, stir in the fruit, eggs and milk. Pour in the syrup mixture and mix well.
3. Pour the mixture into a greased and base-lined 900 g (2 lb) loaf tin.

4. **Baking:** 170°C, 340°F, Gas 3, or fan oven 150°C, for 1–1¹/₂ hours until firm to the touch and golden. Allow to cool in the tin for 5 mins before turning onto a wire rack to cool completely.

CHOCOLATE

ALL-IN-ONE CHOCOLATE CAKE

A quick and easy cake.

170 g (6 oz) self-raising flour
60 ml (4 tbsp) cocoa powder
5 ml (1 tsp) baking powder
115 g (4 oz) light muscovado sugar
15 ml (1 tbsp) black treacle
140 ml (¹/₄ pint) sunflower oil
140 ml (¹/₄ pint) milk
2 medium eggs

For the filling and topping:
340 g (12 oz) fromage frais
60 ml (4 tbsp) blackcurrant jam

1. Place the flour, cocoa, baking powder, sugar, treacle, oil, milk and eggs in a food processor or place in a large bowl and beat with a wooden spoon and blend until the mixture turns creamy.
2. Divide the mixture evenly between two 18 cm (7 ins) greased sandwich tins.

3. **Baking:** 160°C, 320°F, Gas 3, or fan oven 140°C, for 35–45 mins or until just firm to touch. Remove from tins and transfer to a wire rack to cool.

4. Meanwhile, beat together the fromage frais until thickened. When the cakes have cooled, spread one with the jam and smooth over a third of the fromage frais mixture, then carefully sandwich both halves together.
5. Spread the remaining mixture on top of the cake and, using a fork, bring up into peaks. Chill before serving.

CHEWY CHOCOLATE SQUARES

140 g (5 oz) butter
225 g (8 oz) light muscovado sugar
2 medium eggs, beaten
115 g (4 oz) plain flour, sieved
55 g (2 oz) cocoa, sieved
2.5 ml (½ tsp) baking powder, sieved
55 g (2 oz) walnuts, chopped

Icing:
55 g (2 oz) butter
30 ml (2 tbsp) drinking chocolate powder
140 g (5 oz) golden icing sugar, sieved
15 ml (1 tbsp) milk

1. Place the butter in a large saucepan and gently melt, remove from the heat and stir in the sugar and eggs, beat well to mix.
2. Stir in the flour, cocoa, baking powder and walnuts, mix thoroughly.
3. Grease and base line a 20.5 cm (8 ins) square cake tin. Pour the mixture into tin spreading evenly.

4. **Baking:** 180°C, 355°F, Gas 4, or fan oven 160°C, for 35–45 mins until set and springy to touch. Leave to cool in tin before turning onto rack to cool completely.

5. **To make the icing:** In a medium saucepan, melt the butter, then stir in the remaining ingredients and beat until thick. Swirl over the cake.

6. Cut into squares to serve. Ideal for picnics.

MOCHA CAKE

Cake:
170 g (6 oz) plain chocolate
90 ml (6 tbsp) strong black coffee
30 ml (2 tbsp) Tia Maria
85 g (3 oz) dark muscovado sugar
100 g (4 oz) unsalted butter
3 medium eggs, separated
pinch of salt

55 g (2 oz) ground almonds
A few drops of almond essence
55 g (2 oz) plain flour, sifted

Icing:
140 ml (¼ pint) double cream
200 g (7 oz) plain chocolate

1. Melt the chocolate, coffee and Tia Maria over a bowl of simmering water, then allow to cool to room temperature.
2. Reserve a tablespoon of sugar, cream together the remaining sugar and the butter until pale and fluffy.
3. Beat in the egg yolks.

4. Whisk the egg whites and the salt until soft peaks form. Sprinkle on the tablespoon of sugar and then beat the egg whites until stiff peaks are formed.
5. Into the butter and sugar mixture carefully blend the melted chocolate mixture, then stir in the almonds and essence. Gently fold in alternately the flour and egg whites until well blended.
6. Grease and base line a 18 cm (7 ins) cake tin. Turn the mixture into the prepared tin

7. **Baking:** 180°C, 355°F, Gas 4, or fan oven 160°C, for 25–30 mins, until firm to the touch and springy.

8. Allow the cake to cool in the tin for 10 mins before turning out and cooling completely.

9. **To make the icing:** Carefully bring the cream to the boil, remove from the heat and add the chocolate, stirring until melted and well blended. Allow the mixture to cool until it coats the back of a spoon. Spread the mixture over the cake. Place in the fridge to set completely.

CHOCOLATE ALMOND BROWNIES
A variation on American brownies, with a moist and crunchy top.

140 g (5 oz) plain chocolate   **85 g (3 oz) self-raising flour, sieved**
115 g (4 oz) margarine   **55 g (2 oz) ground almonds**
170 g (6 oz) golden caster sugar   **5 ml (1 tsp) almond essence**
5 medium eggs, separated

1. Place the chocolate in a bowl over a pan of simmering water, stir until melted, remove from heat and allow to cool slightly.
2. Beat the margarine and sugar together until light and fluffy, beat in the egg yolks and the melted chocolate until smooth. Stir in the flour, ground almonds and essence.
3. In a clean grease-free bowl, whisk the egg whites until stiff. Using a metal spoon fold into chocolate mixture.
4. Grease and base line a 28 x 18 cm (11 x 7 ins) tin. Spoon mixture into tin.

5. **Baking:** 180°C, 355°F, Gas 4, or fan oven 160°C, for 35–45 mins, until set and springy to the touch. Allow to cool in the tin, then cut into squares to serve.

CHOCOLATE AND BANANA CAKE

A moist cake. For best results use very ripe bananas.

Cake:

170 g (6 oz) margarine	**3 large eggs**
225 g (8 oz) golden granulated sugar	**55 g (2 oz) chocolate chips**
2 large ripe bananas,	
weighing approx. 225 g (8 oz)	
2.5 ml (¹/₂ tsp) vanilla essence	*Crumble topping:*
285 g (10 oz) self-raising flour, sieved	**30 g (1 oz) plain flour**
2.5 ml (¹/₂ tsp) salt	**30 g (1 oz) demerara sugar**
2.5 ml (¹/₂ tsp) bicarbonate of soda	**15 g (¹/₂ oz) butter**

1. Place margarine and sugar in a saucepan, melt over a low heat until just melted. Remove pan from heat.
2. Mash bananas with the vanilla essence.
3. Mix into melted mixture, flour, eggs, bananas and chocolate chips. Gently stir to blend.
4. Grease and line a 20.5 cm (8 ins) deep round cake tin. Place mixture into tin and level top with a spoon.
5. Place the flour and sugar into a bowl, add the butter and rub into mixture until it resembles fine breadcrumbs. Sprinkle onto top of the mixture in the tin.

6. **Baking:** 160°C, 320°F, Gas 3, or fan oven 140°C, for 1¹/₄–1³/₄ hours, until a skewer placed in the centre comes out clean. Leave to cool in the tin for 10 mins before turning out to cool completely.

ORANGE CHOCOLATE DRIZZLE CAKE

170 g (6 oz) margarine	**juice of 1 orange**
170 g (6 oz) golden caster sugar	**30 g (1 oz) golden granulated sugar**
3 medium eggs	
finely grated zest of 1 orange	
170 g (6 oz) self-raising flour	*Icing:*
milk to mix	**115 g (4 oz) plain chocolate**
orange syrup	**15 g (¹/₂ oz) margarine**

1. Cream the margarine and sugar together until light and fluffy. Gradually beat in the eggs with the orange zest.

2. Sieve the flour and fold gently into the mixture, adding enough milk to give a soft dropping consistency.
3. Grease and line a 900 g (2 lb) loaf tin, place prepared mixture in tin, smooth the top, hollowing out the centre a little.

4. **Baking:** 180°C, 355°F, Gas 4, or fan oven 160°C, for 50–75 mins until well risen, firm to the touch and golden. Allow to cool for 5 mins in tin before turning onto cooling rack.

5. **To make the orange syrup:** Strain the orange juice into a saucepan with the sugar and gently heat until dissolved. Carefully spoon over top of cake allowing it to be absorbed.

6. **To make the icing:** Place chocolate in a bowl over hot water to melt then stir in margarine and mix well. Swirl the icing over the top of the cake.

DARK CHOCOLATE CAKE
A tray bake which could be used for afternoon tea.

225 g (8 oz) butter	**4 medium eggs**
170 g (6 oz) light muscovado sugar	**225 g (8 oz) self-raising flour, sieved**
170 g (6 oz) black treacle	**55 g (2 oz) cocoa powder, sieved**

1. Cream the butter, sugar and treacle until light and fluffy, beat in eggs and add a small amount of flour to prevent the mixture from curdling.
2. Fold in the remaining flour and the cocoa powder, mix well.
3. Place the mixture into a greased and base-lined 30.5 x 23 cm (12 x 9 ins) oblong baking tin.

4. **Baking:** 170°C, 340°F, Gas 3, or fan oven 150°C, for 35–50 mins until well risen.

5. Turn onto a wire rack to cool.

Buttercream:
85 g (3 oz) butter
170 g (6 oz) golden icing sugar, sieved

Cream the butter and icing sugar together until smooth and spread over the top of the cake.

DEATH BY CHOCOLATE FUDGE CAKE
The ultimate chocolate cake.

Cake:
140 g (5 oz) butter, softened
225 g (8 oz) dark muscovado sugar
2 medium eggs
140 ml (¼ pint) soured cream
170 g (6 oz) plain flour
5 ml (1 tsp) baking powder
2.5 ml (½ tsp) bicarbonate of soda
55 g (2 oz) cocoa

Filling:
30 ml (2 tbsp) cocoa
140 g (5 oz) butter
170 g (6 oz) icing sugar, sieved
few drops of vanilla essence
Frosting:
200 g (7 oz) plain chocolate
30 ml (2 tbsp) cocoa
140 ml (¼ pint) double cream

1. **For the cake:** cream together the butter and sugar until the mixture is light in colour and texture. Gradually beat in the eggs, and then the soured cream (the mixture will look curdled at this stage).
2. Sieve together the dry ingredients and fold them into the mixture.
3. Grease and base line two 20.5 cm (8 in) sandwich cake tins, divide the mixture equally between the tins.

4. **Baking:** 190°C, 375°F, Gas 5, or fan oven 170°C, for 25–35 mins, until springy to the touch. Turn out onto a wire tray to cool.

5. Make the filling by mixing the cocoa with 30 ml (2 tbsp) of boiling water to a smooth paste; allow to cool.
6. Beat together the butter, sieved icing sugar and essence, until light and fluffy. Beat in cocoa.
7. Slice the cake in half and then sandwich the halves together with the filling.

8. **For the frosting:** Melt the chocolate carefully. Make the cocoa into a paste with water as before, and mix with the chocolate. Slowly whisk the cream into the chocolate until smooth and thickened. Spread the frosting evenly over the cake with a palette knife.

9. Store in fridge. Serve in slices, with whipped cream or ice-cream.

COCONUT AND CHOCOLATE CRUNCH

170 g (6 oz) self-raising flour
pinch of salt
15 ml (1 tbsp) cocoa
140 g (5 oz) margarine

85 g (3 oz) golden caster sugar
115 g (4 oz) desiccated coconut
Topping:
55 g (2 oz) chocolate

1. Sieve the flour, salt and cocoa into a bowl. Rub in the margarine until the mixture resembles fine breadcrumbs.
2. Stir in the sugar and coconut. Knead thoroughly, then press mixture into a lightly greased Swiss roll tin measuring 30.5 x 20.5 cm (12 x 8 ins).

3. **Baking:** 140°C, 285°F, Gas 1, or fan oven 120°C, for 25–35 mins.

4. When cooked allow to cool in tin.

5. **To make topping:** Place the chocolate in a small bowl and place over a pan of hot water to melt. Spread over top of cooled crunch, allow to almost set then cut into fingers, OR place chunks of chocolate over the top of the crunch. Place back in the oven for 1–2 mins to melt the chocolate, spread over the top.

LIGHT CHOCOLATE CAKE

A softer chocolate flavoured cake, by using drinking chocolate powder, which is sweetened with sugar.

170 g (6 oz) soft margarine
170 g (6 oz) golden caster sugar
3 medium eggs
140 g (5 oz) self-raising flour

5 ml (1 tsp) baking powder
85 g (3 oz) drinking chocolate powder
45 ml (3 tbsp) hot water

1. Place all the ingredients except the water in a bowl and beat with a wooden spoon for 2 mins or with a mixer for 1 minute until well blended. Gradually add the water.
2. Grease and line a 23 cm (9 ins) deep round tin. Place mixture in tin and smooth the top.

3. **Baking:** 180°C, 355°F, Gas 4, or fan oven 160°C, for 55–75 mins, until well risen and springy to the touch. Leave to cool in tin before turning onto a rack to cool completely.

FUDGY CHOCOLATE LOAF

170 g (6 oz) butter or margarine
170 g (6 oz) dark muscovado sugar
3 medium eggs
170 g (6 oz) self-raising flour, sieved
55 g (2 oz) cocoa powder, sieved
55 g (2 oz) ground almonds
90 ml (6 tbsp) milk

Frosting:
55 g (2 oz) margarine
45 ml (3 tbsp) milk
225 g (8 oz) golden icing sugar, sieved
30 ml (2 tbsp) cocoa powder, sieved

1. Cream the butter and sugar together until lighter in colour and fluffy. Gradually beat in the eggs.
2. Carefully fold in the flour, cocoa powder and almonds, adding enough milk to give a soft dropping consistency.
3. Grease and base line a 900 g (2 lb) loaf tin, spoon mixture into tin.

4. **Baking:** 170°C, 340°F, Gas 3, or fan oven 150°C, for 55–75 mins until well risen and set. Leave to cool in the tin for 10 mins before turning onto rack to cool completely.

5. **To make frosting:** Place the margarine and milk in a pan and gently melt together, add the icing sugar and cocoa, beat well until smooth. Cool in the fridge until thickened. Spread frosting over top and sides of loaf.

RICH CHOCOLATE CAKE

170 g (6 oz) plain chocolate
115 g (4 oz) butter or margarine
115 g (4 oz) golden caster sugar
4 medium eggs, separated
225 g (8 oz) ground almonds
75 ml (5 tbsp) apricot jam

Topping:
55 g (2 oz) butter
85 g (3 oz) plain chocolate

1. Place the chocolate in a bowl over a pan of simmering water, stir until melted, remove from heat and allow to cool slightly.
2. Cream the butter and sugar together until light and fluffy, beat in the egg yolks and stir in the ground almonds and the melted chocolate, mixing well.
3. Whisk the egg whites until stiff, then fold into chocolate mixture, blending thoroughly.

4. Grease and base line a 20.5 cm (8 ins) spring form tin. Pour mixture into tin, spreading evenly.

5. **Baking:** 180°C, 355°F, Gas 4, or fan oven 160°C, for 45–60 mins until firm to the touch. Leave to cool in the tin for 10 mins before turning onto a rack to cool.

6. Warm apricot jam and brush over top of cake.

7. **Topping:** Place butter and chocolate in a small bowl over a pan of simmering water to melt. Stir and spread over top of cake. Allow to set before serving.

TRADITIONAL AMERICAN BROWNIES
These delectable chocolate squares should be moist inside and chewy.

170 g (6 oz) margarine
30 g (1 oz) cocoa
170 g (6 oz) dark muscovado sugar
2 medium eggs
55 g (2 oz) self-raising flour, sieved
55 g (2 oz) pecan nuts, chopped
115 g (4 oz) chocolate chips

Frosting:
30 g (1 oz) plain chocolate, chopped
45 g (1½ oz) butter
10 ml (2 tsp) cocoa
30 ml (2 tbsp) milk
115 g (4 oz) golden icing sugar, sieved

1. Melt 55 g (2 oz) of margarine in a small saucepan, stir in the cocoa, allow to cool for 5 mins.
2. Cream the remaining margarine with the sugar until lighter in colour and fluffy. Gradually beat in the eggs and the cocoa mixture.
3. Fold in the flour, stir in the nuts and chocolate pieces, mix well.
4. Turn the mixture into a greased and base-lined 18 cm (7 ins) deep square tin.

5. **Baking:** 180°C, 355°F, Gas 4, or fan oven 160°C, for 40–50 mins until well risen and springy.

6. Allow to cool in the tin for 5 mins before turning out onto a rack to cool completely.

7. **To make frosting:** Place the chocolate, butter, cocoa and milk in a small saucepan and melt gently. Remove from heat and beat smooth. Gradually add the icing sugar, beat well until frosting thickens. Spread frosting over brownies. Slice and serve.

SACHERTORTE

Based on the traditional Austrian recipe.

Cake:
225 g (8 oz) plain chocolate
225 g (8 oz) butter
225 g (8 oz) golden caster sugar
5 ml (1 tsp) instant coffee
15 ml (1 tbsp) boiling water
5 medium eggs, separated
170 g (6 oz) self-raising flour, sieved

Filling:
75 ml (5 tbsp) apricot jam
Icing:
170 g (6 oz) plain chocolate
60 ml (4 tbsp) boiling water
15 ml (1 tbsp) coffee liqueur e.g. Tia Maria
170 g (6 oz) golden icing sugar, sieved
To complete:
Melted chocolate for piping

1. Break the chocolate into squares and melt in a bowl over a pan of hot water. Allow to cool.
2. Cream together the butter and sugar until light and fluffy. Dissolve the coffee in the boiling water and stir into the creamed mixture with chocolate. Beat in the egg yolks, one at a time, with a little flour to prevent curdling. Fold in remaining flour.
3. Whisk the egg whites until they form soft peaks, fold gently into the mixture.
4. Grease and line a 23 cm (9 ins) round cake tin. Spoon into the prepared tin and smooth top with a spoon, hollow out centre.

5. **Baking:** 150°C, 300°F, Gas 2, or fan oven 130°C, for $1\frac{1}{4}$–$1\frac{1}{2}$ hours. Leave to cool in the tin for 15 mins and then turn out on to a wire rack to cool completely.

6. When cake has cooled, cut in half horizontally.

7. Warm the apricot jam and sieve to remove lumps. Brush on to one half of the cake and put the other on top. Brush remaining jam over top and sides of cake.

8. **To make the icing:** Melt the chocolate, water and coffee liqueur in a bowl over a pan of hot water. Remove the bowl from the heat and beat in the icing sugar. Spread evenly over cake, using a palette knife dipped into warm water.

9. For the finishing touch you can pipe the word 'Sacher' or 'Sachertorte' on top of the cake in melted chocolate if you wish.

SMALL CAKES

MACAROONS

1 large egg white
115 g (4 oz) golden caster sugar
55 g (2 oz) ground almonds

few drops of almond essence
To decorate:
blanched almonds

1. In a clean grease-free bowl whisk the egg white until stiff. Fold in the caster sugar, ground almonds and essence.
2. Place spoonfuls of the mixture on baking trays lined with non-stick or rice paper. Allow room to spread. Top each with a blanched almond.

3. **Baking:** 180°C, 355°F, Gas 4, or fan oven 160°C, for 20–25 mins until set and just beginning to colour. Cool on a wire rack.

GINGERBREAD HOLLOWS

115 g (4 oz) margarine
340 g (12 oz) golden caster sugar
1 large egg

250 g (9 oz) self-raising flour, sieved
10 ml (2 tsp) ground ginger

1. Cream the margarine and sugar together, blending well.
2. Beat in the egg, and stir in the flour and ginger, work to a pliable dough.
3. Knead gently, roll into balls the size of walnuts. Place apart on greased baking trays.

4. **Baking:** 140°C, 285°F, Gas 1, or fan oven 120°C, for 25–30 mins until just coloured and puffy. Cool on a wire rack.

CHOCOLATE CUP CAKES

These remind me of the cakes my grandmother used to make for Sunday tea.

115 g (4 oz) soft margarine
115 g (4 oz) golden caster sugar
2 medium eggs
115 g (4 oz) self-raising flour
5 ml (1 tsp) baking powder
15 ml (1 tbsp) cocoa powder

Icing:
30 g (1 oz) soft margarine
10 ml (2 tsp) cold water
15 ml (1 tbsp) cocoa powder
115 g (4 oz) golden icing sugar

1. Place the margarine, sugar and eggs into a bowl, sieve the flour, baking powder and cocoa into the bowl. Beat together with a wooden spoon for 2–3 mins until well mixed.
2. Stand 18 paper cases on baking sheet or bun tins. Half fill with cake mixture.

3. **Baking:** 190°C, 375°F, Gas 5, or fan oven 170°C, for 15–20 mins until well risen and firm to the touch. Cool on a wire rack.

4. **To make the icing:** Melt the margarine, water and cocoa in a bowl over hot water. Remove from the heat and beat in the icing sugar until smooth and shiny. Place a spoonful of the icing on the top of each cake and spread evenly.

SWISS WHIRLS

225 g (8 oz) butter
2–3 drops vanilla essence
225 g (8 oz) plain flour, sieved
pinch of salt

55 g (2 oz) golden icing sugar
a little raspberry jam
icing sugar to finish

1. Soften the butter with a wooden spoon, beat in the vanilla essence. Gradually beat in the flour, salt and icing sugar, beating well after each addition. Continue beating until well blended and quite a soft consistency.
2. Place the mixture in a piping bag fitted with a medium-sized fluted nozzle. Place paper cases into 12 bun tins. Starting at the centre of each case, pipe a spiral towards the outside, leaving a slight well in the centre.

3. **Baking:** 200°C, 390°F, Gas 6, or fan oven 180°C, for 10–15 mins to lightly brown.

4. Place on a wire rack to cool. When cold, fill the centre of each whirl with a little raspberry jam and dredge with icing sugar.

COCONUT BUNS

These are ideal for packed lunch.

115 g (4 oz) soft margarine
115 g (4 oz) golden caster sugar
2 medium eggs

115 g (4 oz) self-raising flour, sieved
5 ml (1 tsp) baking powder, sieved
55 g (2 oz) desiccated coconut

1. Place all the ingredients in a mixing bowl and beat together with a wooden spoon for 2–3 mins until well blended.
2. Divide the mixture evenly between 14–16 paper cases placed in bun tins or on baking trays.

3. **Baking:** 190°C, 375°F, Gas 5, or fan oven 170°C, for 15–20 mins until risen and lightly browned. Cool on a wire rack.

LEMON BUTTERFLY CAKES

115 g (4 oz) margarine
115 g (4 oz) light muscovado sugar
2 medium eggs
15 ml (1 tbsp) golden syrup
170 g (6 oz) self-raising flour, sieved
7.5 ml (1$\frac{1}{2}$ tsp) ground ginger, sieved
grated zest of $\frac{1}{2}$ lemon
30 ml (2 tbsp) lemon juice

Icing:
115 g (4 oz) margarine
170 g (6 oz) golden icing sugar, sieved
grated zest and juice of $\frac{1}{2}$ lemon

1. Cream the margarine and sugar together in a bowl until light and fluffy.
2. Beat in the eggs and the golden syrup. Fold in the flour and ginger, stir in the lemon zest and juice and mix well.
3. Divide spoonfuls of the mixture between cake cases on a baking tray.

4. **Baking:** 190°C, 375°F, Gas 5, or fan oven 170°C, for 15–25 mins until firm to the touch and golden. Leave to cool on a wire rack.

5. **To make the icing:** Cream the margarine and icing sugar together until creamy, stir in the lemon zest and juice. Place the icing in a piping bag fitted with a star nozzle.

6. Cut a thin slice off top of each cake, cut each slice in half. Pipe a swirl of icing on top of each cake. Place the half slices back at an angle to resemble wings.

MADELEINES

These traditional tea time treats are easy to make and look delightful.

115 g (4 oz) margarine
115 g (4 oz) golden caster sugar
2 medium eggs
115 g (4 oz) self-raising flour

Decoration:
raspberry jam, sieved
desiccated coconut
glacé cherries

1. Cream the margarine and sugar together until light and fluffy. Add the eggs, one at a time, beating well.
2. Sieve the flour and gently fold into mixture.
3. Lightly grease 12 dariole moulds and divide mixture between moulds, place on a baking sheet.

4. **Baking:** 190°C, 375°F, Gas 5, or fan oven 170°C, for 12–18 mins until firm to the touch and golden brown. Leave to cool for 5 mins before turning onto a cooling rack.

5. **To decorate:** Warm the jam, brush onto each cake, then roll in the coconut and top with a half of a cherry.

RASPBERRY BUNS

I remember making these at school, learning the whole process of cooking, baking and tidying up.

225 g (8 oz) self-raising flour
pinch of salt
85 g (3 oz) margarine

85 g (3 oz) golden caster sugar
2 medium eggs
raspberry jam

1. Sieve the flour and salt into a mixing bowl and rub in the margarine until the mixture resembles fine breadcrumbs.
2. Stir in sugar, make a well in centre, add eggs and mix well to form stiff dough.
3. Turn onto a lightly floured surface and form into a roll. Cut into 10 pieces and shape into balls.
4. Place on lightly greased baking tray.
5. Make a hole in the middle of each and fill with a little raspberry jam, close the hole carefully and dust tops with a little sugar.

6. **Baking:** 200°C, 390°F, Gas 6, or fan oven 180°C, for 15–20 mins until golden brown. Cool on a wire rack. Best eaten fresh.

MINI PASSION CAKES

140 g (5 oz) butter, melted
200 g (7 oz) light muscovado sugar
115 g (4 oz) finely grated carrots
55 g (2 oz) peeled and finely
    grated eating apples
pinch of salt
5 ml (1 tsp) ground mixed spice
2 medium eggs
200 g (7 oz) self-raising flour
10 ml (2 tsp) baking powder
115 g (4 oz) walnuts, chopped

Topping:
170 g (6 oz) low-fat soft cheese
60–75 ml (4–5 tbsp) single cream
55 g (2 oz) golden icing sugar, sieved

To finish:
30 g (1 oz) walnut halves
10 ml (2 tsp) cocoa powder

1. Arrange 24 paper fairy cake cases in bun tins.
2. Place butter, sugar, carrots, apples, salt, mixed spice and eggs in a bowl and beat together.
3. Sieve flour and baking powder and fold gently into the creamed mixture. Add walnuts and fold in until evenly blended.
4. Fill the paper cases half-full with the mixture.

5. **Baking:** 180°C, 355°F, Gas 4, or fan oven 160°C, for 20–25 mins, or until a skewer inserted into a cake comes out clean.

6. Leave the cakes in the tins for about 5 mins before transferring them to a wire rack to cool completely.

7. **To make the topping:** Stir together soft cheese, cream and icing sugar in a bowl until smooth. Spoon a little in the centre of each cake and decorate with a walnut half. Dust with cocoa and allow the icing to set before serving.

8. To make one big cake, which serves 6–8 people, use a 20.5 cm (8 ins) fluted tin and bake for 1–1¼ hours. Leave to cool before turning out.

ROCK CAKES

'Rocky' shaped fruit buns.

225 g (8 oz) plain flour
10 ml (2 tsp) baking powder
pinch of salt
5 ml (1 tsp) mixed spice
115 g (4 oz) margarine

85 g (3 oz) demerara sugar
115 g (4 oz) mixed dried fruit
1 medium egg
5–10 ml (1–2 tsp) milk

1. Sieve the flour, baking powder, salt and spice into a mixing bowl, rub in the margarine until the mixture resembles breadcrumbs.
2. Stir in the sugar and fruit. Make a well in the centre and beat in the egg and enough milk to give a stiff crumbly consistency.
3. Place rough spoonfuls of the mixture onto lightly greased baking trays. Makes about 12.

4. **Baking:** 200°C, 390°F, Gas 6, or fan oven 180°C, for 15–20 mins, until lightly browned. Best eaten fresh.

Variation: Replace fruit with diced, ready-to-eat dried apricots and chopped glacé cherries.

SMALL CAKES

These are known as Queen's cakes as well.

170 g (6 oz) butter or margarine
170 g (6 oz) golden caster sugar

3 medium eggs
170 g (6 oz) self-raising flour, sieved

1. Cream the butter and sugar together until light and fluffy. Add the eggs beating well. If necessary add a little flour to prevent curdling.
2. Fold in the remaining flour and mix well.
3. Divide mixture evenly between 20–24 paper cases placed on baking trays.

4. **Baking:** 190°C, 375°F, Gas 5, or fan oven 170°C, for 15–25 mins until well risen and golden.

Variations: Add one of the following after the flour, stir in gently.
    85 g (3 oz) chopped glacé cherries
    85 g (3 oz) chocolate chips
    85 g (3 oz) sultanas

MISCELLANEOUS

COFFEE PECAN BARS
These moist bars are delicious.

225 g (8 oz) butter, softened
225 g (8 oz) light muscovado sugar
4 medium eggs
225 g (8 oz) self-raising flour
10 ml (2 tsp) cinnamon
115 g (4 oz) pecan nuts,
    roughly chopped

Syrup:
285 ml ($^1/_2$ pint) strong black coffee
85 g (3 oz) golden granulated sugar
45 ml (3 tbsp) Tia Maria liqueur

Topping:
30 g (1 oz) demerara sugar
55 g (2 oz) pecan nuts, chopped

1. Beat together butter, sugar, eggs, flour, cinnamon and nuts until well blended.
2. Spoon the mixture into a greased and base-lined 23 cm (9 ins) square tin.

3. **Baking:** 180°C, 355°F, Gas 4, or fan oven 160°C, for 30–45 mins until well risen and firm to the touch. Allow to cool in the tin.

4. **To make syrup:** Place the coffee and sugar in a saucepan, gently heat to dissolve the sugar. Boil for about 10–15 mins until syrupy. Add the coffee liqueur and cool. Drizzle over the top of the cake. Sprinkle with sugar and pecan nuts.

5. Cut into rectangles to serve.

CHERRY AND APRICOT SCONES

The fruit makes these very colourful scones.

450 g (1 lb) plain flour
10 ml (2 tsp) cream of tartar
5 ml (1 tsp) bicarbonate of soda
115 g (4 oz) block margarine
55 g (2 oz) golden caster sugar

85 g (3 oz) no-need-to-soak dried
  apricots, chopped
85 g (3 oz) glacé cherries, chopped
225 ml (8 fl oz) milk

1. Sift together flour, cream of tartar and bicarbonate of soda.
2. Rub in margarine until mixture resembles fine breadcrumbs.
3. Stir in sugar, chopped cherries and apricots, mix well.
4. Stir in enough milk to give a fairly soft dough.
5. Turn onto lightly floured surface, knead lightly. Roll out to about 2 cm ($^3/_4$ inch). Cut into 6.5 cm ($2^1/_2$ ins) rounds. Place on baking sheet. Knead remaining dough and re-roll.

6. **Baking:** In a pre-heated oven at 230°C, 445°F, Gas 8, for 10–20 mins, or fan oven 210°C, for 10–15 mins, until well risen and golden brown.

SCONES

Traditional recipe, served with jam and cream.

450 g (1 lb) plain flour
10 ml (2 tsp) cream of tartar
5 ml (1 tsp) bicarbonate of soda

115 g (4 oz) block margarine
225 ml (8 fl oz) milk

1. Sift together flour, cream of tartar and bicarbonate of soda.
2. Rub in margarine until mixture resembles fine breadcrumbs.
3. Make a well in centre. Stir in enough milk to give fairly soft dough.
4. Turn onto lightly floured surface. Knead lightly to remove any cracks. Roll out to about 2 cm ($^3/_4$ inch). Cut out 5 cm (2 ins) rounds. Place on baking sheet.
5. Knead remaining dough and re-roll.

6. **Baking:** In a pre-heated oven at 230°C, 445°F, Gas 8, or fan oven 210°C, for 10–15 mins, until well risen and golden brown.

Note: Use a plain cutter for savoury scones and a fluted cutter for sweet scones.

ORANGE AND LEMON BARS

Flapjack style bars, ideal for lunch boxes.

zest of 1 orange, finely grated
zest of 1 lemon, finely grated
225 g (8 oz) butter
225 g (8 oz) golden caster sugar
170 g (6 oz) golden syrup

395 g (14 oz) rolled oats
115 g (4 oz) raisins
115 g (4 oz) ready-to-eat apricots, chopped
30 g (1 oz) sunflower seeds

1. In a large saucepan place the orange and lemon zest, butter, sugar and syrup. Gently heat, stirring until melted.
2. Remove from the heat and stir in the remaining ingredients, mixing well.
3. Place in an oiled and base-lined 20.5 x 30.5 cm (8 x 12 ins) shallow tin.

4. **Baking:** 180°C, 355°F, Gas 4, or fan oven 160°C, for 20–30 mins until set and golden in colour.

5. Remove from oven, mark into bars and leave to cool. When cold, break into bars and store in airtight container.

APRICOT AND COCONUT BARS

These are great for picnics.

170 g (6 oz) ready-to-eat apricots
45 ml (3 tbsp) orange juice
170 g (6 oz) margarine
30 ml (2 tbsp) golden syrup
85 g (3 oz) plain flour

1.25 ml ($^1/_4$ tsp) bicarbonate of soda
85 g (3 oz) desiccated coconut
115 g (4 oz) rolled oats
170 g (6 oz) demerara sugar
grated zest of 1 orange

1. Place the apricots and orange juice in a saucepan and bring juice to the boil, remove from the heat and leave to cool. Purée in a blender.
2. In a saucepan melt the margarine and syrup together. Remove from the heat and stir in the flour, bicarbonate of soda, coconut, oats, sugar and orange zest, mixing well.
3. Spoon half the mixture into a greased and base-lined 20.5 cm (8 ins) square tin. Spread the apricot purée over and smooth with a knife, then top with the remaining coconut mixture. Smooth the top.

4. **Baking:** 190°C, 375°F, Gas 5, or fan oven 170°C, for 30–40 mins until set and golden brown. Mark into bars and cut when cold.

TEA TIME FRUITY SQUARES

225 g (8 oz) wholemeal self-raising flour
pinch of salt
115 g (4 oz) margarine   *Topping:*
5 ml (1 tsp) cinnamon   15 ml (1 tbsp) milk
85 g (3 oz) golden caster sugar   15 ml (1 tbsp) demerara sugar
85 g (3 oz) sultanas   5 ml (1 tsp) cinnamon
85 g (3 oz) glacé cherries, chopped
45–75 ml (3–5 tbsp) milk

1. Sieve the flour and salt into a bowl. Rub the margarine into the flour until the mixture resembles fine breadcrumbs.
2. Add spice, sugar and fruit, mix well, stir in enough milk to form a stiff dough.
3. On a lightly floured surface, knead dough and roll out to fit a 28 x 23 cm (11 x 9 ins) baking tin. Brush top with milk and sprinkle with sugar and spice.

4. **Baking:** 220°C, 430°F, Gas 7, or fan oven 200°C, for 15–20 mins until well risen and golden. Serve cut in squares.

GINGER SLICE

340 g (12 oz) plain wholemeal flour   *Icing:*
115 g (4 oz) light muscovado sugar   85 g (3 oz) margarine
170 g (6 oz) margarine   170 g (6 oz) light muscovado sugar
55 g (2 oz) stem ginger, finely chopped   5 ml (1 tsp) ground ginger

1. Place the flour and sugar in a bowl and mix together. Melt the margarine and, with the ginger, pour into the flour, mixing well.
2. Press mixture into lightly greased 29 x 19 cm (11½ x 7½ ins) Swiss roll tin in an even layer.

3. **Baking:** 180°C, 355°F, Gas 4, or fan oven 160°C, for 20–30 mins. until just firm to the touch.

4. **For the icing:** Place the margarine, sugar and ginger into a small saucepan and heat gently, stirring continuously, until all the sugar is dissolved. Bring to the boil and *without stirring* boil until the mixture leaves the sides of the pan.
5. Remove from the heat and beat until the mixture thickens and loses its shine.
6. Pour on the top of the warm shortbread and spread evenly. Allow to cool in the tin, cut into fingers to serve.

TRADITIONAL

VICTORIA SANDWICH

115 g (4 oz) block margarine   2 medium eggs
115 g (4 oz) golden caster sugar   115 g (4 oz) self raising flour

1. Cream margarine and sugar until light, fluffy and pale colour.
2. Beat in eggs. Sift flour and fold into mixture.
3. Grease and base line two 18 cm (7 ins) sandwich tins. Divide mixture equally into tins. Level tops.

4. **Baking:** 180°C, 355°F, Gas 4, or fan oven 160°C, for 20–30 mins until well risen, golden brown and springy to the touch.

5. Allow to cool. Turn cake onto a tea towel first and then back onto a cooling rack to avoid marks on top surface. Sandwich together with raspberry or apricot jam. Sprinkle top of cake with caster sugar.

ALL-IN-ONE VICTORIA SANDWICH

115 g (4 oz) soft margarine   115 g (4 oz) self-raising flour, sieved
115 g (4 oz) golden caster sugar   5 ml (1 tsp) baking powder, sieved
2 medium eggs

1. Place all ingredients in a bowl, beat with a wooden spoon for 2 mins or with an electric mixer for 1 minute.
2. Grease and base line two 18 cm (7 ins) sandwich tins. Divide mixture equally into tins. Level tops.

3. **Baking:** 170°C, 340°F, Gas 3, or fan oven 150°C, for 20–30 mins until well risen, golden brown and springy to the touch.

4. Allow to cool. Follow instructions as for 5 above, VICTORIA SANDWICH.

COFFEE AND WALNUT CAKE

Cake:
55 g (2 oz) walnuts, finely chopped
170 g (6 oz) self-raising flour
5 ml (1 tsp) baking powder
170 g (6 oz) butter, softened
85 g (3 oz) light muscovado sugar
85 g (3 oz) golden caster sugar
3 medium eggs
15 ml (1 tbsp) coffee essence

Icing:
15 ml (1 tbsp) coffee powder
30 ml (2 tbsp) boiling water
225 g (8 oz) golden icing sugar
140 g (5 oz) butter

To finish:
55 g (2 oz) walnut halves

1. Sieve the flour and baking powder into a mixing bowl, add all the cake ingredients and beat together with a wooden spoon for 2 mins or an electric mixer for 1 minute until thoroughly blended.
2. Divide the mixture evenly between two greased and base-lined 18 cm (7 ins) sandwich tins, level the tops.

3. **Baking:** 180°C, 355°F, Gas 4, or fan oven 160°C, for 25–35 mins until the cakes are risen, springy to the touch and golden.

4. Leave in the tins for 5 mins before turning onto a wire rack, remove the greaseproof paper and leave to cool completely.

5. **To make the icing:** In a bowl mix the coffee powder and boiling water, allow to cool. Add the sieved icing sugar and butter, beat until smooth.

6. Spread half of the icing over half of the cake, sandwich together and spread remaining icing on top of cake and decorate with the walnut halves.

SPONGE CAKES
These mixtures contain no fat, but a high proportion of eggs and sugar, and are made by the 'Whisking' method. If whisking by hand it should be carried out with the bowl standing over a pan of hot water; however, if using an electric mixer, no heat is required during whisking.

Basic sponge cake:
3 medium eggs
115 g (4 oz) golden caster sugar
85 g (3 oz) plain flour

1. Put the eggs and sugar in a deep bowl and whisk together until the mixture is thick enough to retain a trail of the whisk.
2. Sift half the flour into the mixture, fold in very carefully using a metal spoon, repeat with remaining flour.
3. Pour the mixture evenly between two 18 cm (7 ins) sandwich tins which have been greased and dusted with a mixture of flour and caster sugar. Tilt the mixture in the tins to spread evenly.

4. **Baking:** 190°C, 375°F, Gas 5, or pre-heated fan oven 170°C, for 15–20 mins until risen and pale golden.

5. Turn out onto a wire rack to cool.
6. Sandwich together with jam and dust top with golden caster sugar to serve.

SWISS ROLL

3 medium eggs	*To finish:*
85 g (3 oz) golden caster sugar	**jam**
85 g (3 oz) plain flour	**golden caster sugar**
15 ml (1 tbsp) hot water	

1. Put the eggs and sugar in a deep bowl and whisk together until the mixture is thick enough to retain a trail of the whisk.
2. Sift half the flour into the mixture, fold in very carefully using a metal spoon, repeat with remaining flour. Lightly stir in the water.
3. Pour the mixture into a greased and lined 30.5 x 23 cm (12 x 9 ins) Swiss roll tin, tilting tin to spread the mixture evenly in the tin.

4. **Baking:** 210°C, 410°F, Gas 6 or pre-heated fan oven 190°C, for 10–20 mins until well risen, spongy and golden brown.

5. Have ready a sheet of greaseproof paper liberally sprinkled with caster sugar. Turn the cooked sponge onto the paper, remove the greaseproof paper from the base, trim the edges and spread the surface with warmed jam. Roll up making the first turn firmly so the finished cake has a good shape.
6. Dredge the cake with golden caster sugar, cool on a wire rack.

To make a Chocolate Swiss Roll: Replace 30 g (1 oz) of flour with cocoa powder.

CHARTS

TEMPERATURE CONVERSION CHART

The temperature equivalents below have been used throughout this book.

Note that temperatures vary slightly between every oven, and most ovens will indicate temperature only to the nearest 10°. Fahrenheit temperatures have been rounded to the nearest 5°F so that cooks can start with an accurate conversion and make their own compensations as they judge best.

Gas mark	Conventional oven °C	°F	Fan °C
1/2	120	250	100
1/2	130	265	110
1	140	285	120
2	150	300	130
3	160	320	140
3	170	340	150
4	180	355	160
5	190	375	170
6	200	390	180
6	210	410	190
7	220	430	200
8	230	445	210
9	240	465	220

Oven pre-heating may not be necessary for most recipes.

Guidelines for fan oven cooking:

1. DO NOT pre-heat the oven except for sensitive mixtures which need hot air immediately they are placed in the oven, i.e. bread, scones, Yorkshire pudding, soufflés, whisked sponges.
2. Reduce the conventional oven cooking temperature that is recommended by 20°C.
3. Reduce the recommended cooking time by 10 mins in the hour.

SPECIAL OCCASIONS CAKES

Ingredients: see charts on following pages 68 and 69

Method:

1. Weigh out fruit.
2. Weigh out and sieve flour, add spices, lemon rind and ground almonds.
3. Cream butter and sugar together until lighter in colour and fluffy.
4. Beat in eggs, one at a time. Add a little flour to stop curdling.
5. Fold in the flour mixture, then gently add the fruit, ensuring it is mixed thoroughly.
6. Place into prepared tin, smooth top and hollow out centre a little.

Baking: 140–150°C, 285–300°F, Gas 1–2. or fan oven 120–130°C, for the time given on the chart.

Note: When baking large cakes – 25.5 cm (10 in) and upwards – reduce the oven heat to 130°C, 265°F, Gas 1 after two-thirds of the cooking time.

WEDDING CAKES

It is important for the final overall result to choose sizes of tiers carefully, avoiding a combination that would look too heavy. Good proportions for a three tier cake are 30.5 cm (12 ins), 23 cm (9 ins) and 15 cm (6 ins); for a two tier cake 30.5 cm (12 ins) and 20.5 cm (8 ins), 28 cm (11 ins) and 18 cm (7 ins) or 25.5 cm (10 ins) and 15 cm (6 ins).

The bottom tier should be deeper than the upper ones, therefore cakes of 25.5–30.5 cm (10–12 ins) diameter are generally about 7.5 cm (3 ins) deep, whilst those 18–23 cm (7–9 ins) are 6.5 cm (2½ ins) deep, and 15 cm (6 ins) diameter cakes are 5 cm (2 ins) deep.

For a three tier cake, bake the two smaller cakes together, and the largest one should be baked separately.

Bake the cakes 2–3 months before the wedding. When they are cold, prick at intervals with a fine skewer and spoon some brandy evenly over the surface. Wrap cakes in greaseproof paper and then in double thickness foil. Store in a cool, dry place.

SPECIAL OCCASIONS CAKES
(see method page 67, and chart page 69 opposite)

Square tin (side)	12.5 cm (5 ins)	15 cm (6 ins)	18 cm (7 ins)	20.5 cm (8 ins)	23 cm (9 ins)	25.5 cm (10 ins)	28 cm (11 ins)	30.5 cm (12 ins)	33 cm (13 ins)
Round tin (diameter)	15 cm (6 ins)	18 cm (7 ins)	20.5 cm (8 ins)	23 cm (9 ins)	25.5 cm (10 ins)	28 cm (11 ins)	30.5 cm (12 ins)	33 cm (13 ins)	35.5 cm (14 ins)
approx. liquid capacity of mix.	570 ml (1 pint)	1 litre (1¾ pints)	1.4 litres (2½ pints)	1.8 litres (3¼ pints)	3.7 litres (6½ pints)	4.1 litres (7¼ pints)	4.5 litres (8 pints)	6 litres (10½ pints)	6.5 litres (11½ pints)
approx. weight (cooked)	900 g (2 lb)	1.1 kg (2½ lb)	1.6 kg (3½ lb)	2 kg (4½ lb)	2.7 kg (6 lb)	4.1 kg (9 lb)	5.2 kg (11½ lb)	6.8 kg (15 lb)	7.7 kg (17 lb)
INGREDIENTS									
Currants	200 g (7 oz)	225 g (8 oz)	340 g (12 oz)	395 g (14 oz)	625 g (1 lb 6 oz)	795 g (1 lb 12 oz)	1.1 kg (2 lb 8 oz)	1.5 kg (3 lb 4 oz)	1.7 kg (3 lb 12 oz)
Sultanas	85 g (3 oz)	115 g (4 oz)	130 g (4 1/2 oz)	170 g (6 oz)	225 g (8 oz)	370 g (13 oz)	395 g (14 oz)	540 g (1 lb 3 oz)	625 g (1 lb 6 oz)
Raisins (seedless)	85 g (3 oz)	115 g (4 oz)	130 g (4 1/2 oz)	170 g (6 oz)	225 g (8 oz)	370 g (13 oz)	395 g (14 oz)	540 g (1 lb 3 oz)	625 g (1 lb 6 oz)
Glacé cherries	55 g (2 oz)	55 g (2 oz)	85 g (3 oz)	130 g (4 1/2 oz)	170 g (6 oz)	250 g (9 oz)	285 g (10 oz)	340 g (12 oz)	425 g (15 oz)
Mixed peel	30 g (1 oz)	30 g (1 oz)	55 g (2 oz)	85 g (3 oz)	115 g (4 oz)	140 g (5 oz)	200 g (7 oz)	250 g (9 oz)	285 g (10 oz)

SPECIAL OCCASIONS CAKES (continued)
(see method page 67, and chart page 68 opposite)

Almonds (flaked)	30 g (1 oz)	30 g (1 oz)	55 g (2 oz)	85 g (3 oz)	115 g (4 oz)	140 g (5 oz)	200 g (7 oz)	250 g (9 oz)	285 g (10 oz)
Lemon rind	a little	a little	a little	a little	¼ lemon	¼ lemon	½ lemon	½ lemon	1 lemon
Plain flour	140 g (5 oz)	170 g (6 oz)	200 g (7 oz)	310 g (11 oz)	395 g (14 oz)	595 g (1 lb 5 oz)	680 g (1 lb 8 oz)	820 g (1 lb 13 oz)	1075 g (2 lb 6 oz)
Mixed spice	1.25 ml (¼ tsp)	1.25 ml (¼ tsp)	2.5 ml (½ level tsp)	2.5 ml (½ level tsp)	5 ml (1 level tsp)	5 ml (1 level tsp)	10 ml (2 level tsp)	12.5 ml (2½ level tsp)	12.5 ml (2½ level tsp)
Cinnamon	1.25 ml (¼ tsp)	1.25 ml (¼ tsp)	2.5 ml (½ level tsp)	2.5 ml (½ level tsp)	5 ml (1 level tsp)	5 ml (1 level tsp)	10 ml (2 level tsp)	12.5 ml (2½ level tsp)	12.5 ml (2½ level tsp)
Butter	130 g (4½ oz)	140 g (5 oz)	170 g (6 oz)	250 g (9 oz)	340 g (12 oz)	510 g (1 lb 2 oz)	595 g (1 lb 5 oz)	795 g (1 lb 12 oz)	950 g (2 lb 2 oz)
Molasses sugar	130 g (4½ oz)	140 g (5 oz)	170 g (6 oz)	250 g (9 oz)	340 g (12 oz)	510 g (1 lb 2 oz)	595 g (1 lb 5 oz)	795 g (1 lb 12 oz)	950 g (2 lb 2 oz)
Eggs (medium)	2	2½	3	4	6	9	11	14	17
Brandy	15 ml (1 tbsp)	15 ml (1 tbsp)	15 ml (1 tbsp)	15–30 ml (1–2 tbsp)	30 ml (2 tbsp)	30–45 ml (2–3 tbsp)	45 ml (3 tbsp)	60 ml (4 tbsp)	90 ml (6 tbsp)
Cooking time (approx.)	2½ hrs	2½–3 hrs	3 hrs	3½ hrs	4 hrs	5½ hrs	7 hrs	8 hrs	8½ hrs

MADEIRA CAKE

Ingredients: see chart on facing page 71

The chart indicates the quantities of ingredients required to make Madeira cakes to fit the standard range of square and round tins. If you want to make a shaped cake, such as a number or heart, you need to know how much mixture is required to fill the special tin. This is quite simple to calculate. Simply fill the tin with water, to the depth you require the cake to be, and measure the water. Then look on the chart.

Method:

1. Soften the butter, add the sugar. Cream together until pale and fluffy.
2. Sift together the flours.
3. Beat the eggs – one at a time – into the creamed mixture. If it looks to be curdling add 15–30 ml (1–2 tbsp) flour.
4. Fold in the remaining flour with the grated lemon rind and juice.
5. Line tin base and sides with baking parchment. Turn into the prepared tin and level the top.
6. Bake at 170°C, 340°F, Gas 3, or 150°C, fan oven, for the time given on the chart.
7. Allow to cool in the tin for 5–10 mins then turn out on a wire rack to cool completely.

LINING A DEEP CAKE TIN

The finished appearance of a cake depends on the careful preparation of a cake tin.

1. Cut a strip of greaseproof or silicone paper to fit around the sides of the tin; this strip should be at least 5 cm (2 ins) wider than the depth of the tin.
2. Make a fold about 2.5 cm (1 inch) along one long edge of the strip. Cut at intervals at slight angles along this edge.
3. Lightly grease the insides of the tin and place the strip around the sides and base of the tin, overlapping the edges.
4. Cut a piece of greaseproof or silicone paper to fit the base.
5. Lightly grease the inside base of the tin and place paper in tin. Lightly grease the lining paper.

Square tin (side)	12.5 cm (5 ins)	15 cm (6 ins)	18 cm (7 ins)	20.5 cm (8 ins)	23 cm (9 ins)	25.5 cm (10 ins)	28 cm (11 ins)	30.5 cm (12 ins)
Round tin (diameter)	15 cm (6 ins)	18 cm (7 ins)	20.5 cm (8 ins)	23 cm (9 ins)	25.5 cm (10 ins)	28 cm (11 ins)	30.5 cm (12 ins)	33 cm (13 ins)
approx. liquid capacity of finished cake	285 ml ($1/2$ pint)	710 ml ($1^{1/4}$ pint)	1 litre ($1^{3/4}$ pint)	1.4 litres ($2^{1/2}$ pint)	1.8 litres ($3^{1/4}$ pint)	2.1 litres ($3^{3/4}$ pint)	2.6 litres ($4^{1/2}$ pint)	3 litres ($5^{1/4}$ pint)
INGREDIENTS								
Butter	55 g (2 oz)	115 g (4 oz)	170 g (6 oz)	225 g (8 oz)	285 g (10 oz)	340 g (12 oz)	395 g (14 oz)	450 g (1 lb)
Golden caster sugar	55 g (2 oz)	115 g (4 oz)	170 g (6 oz)	225 g (8 oz)	285 g (10 oz)	340 g (12 oz)	395 g (14 oz)	450 g (1 lb)
Self-raising flour	55 g (2 oz)	115 g (4 oz)	170 g (6 oz)	225 g (8 oz)	285 g (10 oz)	340 g (12 oz)	395 g (14 oz)	450 g (1 lb)
Plain flour	30 g (1 oz)	55 g (2 oz)	85 g (3 oz)	115 g (4 oz)	140 g (5 oz)	170 g (6 oz)	200 g (7 oz)	225 g (8 oz)
Eggs (medium)	1	2	3	4	5	6	7	8
Grated lemon rind and juice	$1/4$ lemon	$1/2$ lemon	1 lemon	1 lemon	$1^{1/2}$ lemons	$1^{1/2}$ lemons	2 lemons	2 lemons
Cooking time (approx.)	35–45 mins	1 hr – $1^{1/4}$ hrs	$1^{1/4}$ hrs – $1^{1/2}$ hrs	$1^{1/4}$ hrs – $1^{1/2}$ hrs	$1^{1/4}$ hrs – $1^{1/2}$ hrs	$1^{1/4}$ hrs – $1^{1/2}$ hrs	$1^{1/4}$ hrs – $1^{1/2}$ hrs	1 hr 20 m. – 1 hr 40 m.

MOIST CHOCOLATE CAKE

Ingredients: see chart on facing page 73

The chart is designed to allow you to make any round or square cake for a special occasion using this moist dark chocolate cake.

Method:

1. Mix the cocoa and the boiling water together slowly until smooth. Leave to cool completely.
2. Cream the butter and sugar together until lighter in colour and fluffy.
3. Sift flour, bicarbonate of soda and baking powder together. Gradually beat in eggs into creamed mixture, adding some flour to avoid any curdling of mixture.
4. Gently fold in the cocoa mixture with the remaining flour. Mix thoroughly until an even colour is achieved.
5. Pour the mixture into the prepared tin and cook at 180°C, 355°F, Gas 4, or fan oven 160°C, for the time specified in the chart.
6. Insert a skewer in centre of cake; the cake is cooked when it comes out clean.
7. When the cake is cooked remove from the oven, allow to cool in the tin for 15 mins, then turn tin upside down onto a cooling rack and leave to cool completely. This will give a level finish to the cake.
8. If cake is to be stored for more than 7 days, freeze until required.

BUTTERCREAM

115 g (4 oz) softened butter
285 g (10 oz) sieved golden icing sugar

Cream together the butter and sugar until well mixed and smooth. Use as a filling or topping.

VARIATIONS:
1. To make orange (or lemon) flavoured, add finely grated zest of orange (or lemon) and 30 ml (2 tbsp) orange juice (or lemon juice).
2. Stir in 30 ml (2 tbsp) runny honey.
3. Stir in 30 ml (2 tbsp) thick yoghurt.
4. To make chocolate flavoured, dissolve 30 ml (2 tbsp) sieved cocoa powder in 60 ml (4 tbsp) boiling water, mix to a smooth paste, allow to cool, then beat into icing.

Round tin	15 cm (6 ins)	18 cm (7 ins)	20.5 cm (8 ins)	23 cm (9 ins)	25.5 cm (10 ins)	28 cm (11 ins)	30.5 cm (12 ins)	30.5 cm (12 ins)
Square tin		15 cm (6 ins)	18 cm (7 ins)	20.5 cm (8 ins)	23 cm (9 ins)	25.5 cm (10 ins)	28 cm (11 ins)	
INGREDIENTS								
Cocoa	30 g (1 oz)	55 g (2 oz)	85 g (3 oz)	115 g (4 oz)	140 g (5 oz)	170 g (6 oz)	200 g (7 oz)	225 g (8 oz)
Boiling water	90 ml (6 tbsp)	170 ml (6 fl oz)	285 ml (10 fl oz)	370 ml (13 fl oz)	510 ml (18 fl oz)	595 ml (21 fl oz)	680 ml (24 fl oz)	765 ml (27 fl oz)
Butter	115 g (4 oz)	200 g (7 oz)	250 g (9 oz)	310 g (11 oz)	370 g (13 oz)	450 g (1 lb)	565 g (1 lb 4 oz)	710 g (1 lb 9 oz)
Light muscavado sugar	285 g (10 oz)	425 g (15 oz)	565 g (1 lb 4 oz)	710 g (1 lb 9 oz)	850 g (1 lb 14 oz)	990 g (2 lb 3 oz)	1275 g (2 lb 13 oz)	1560 g (3 lb 7 oz)
Plain flour	200 g (7 oz)	310 g (11 oz)	395 g (14 oz)	510 g (1 lb 2 oz)	595 g (1 lb 5 oz)	680 g (1 lb 8 oz)	900 g (2 lb)	1075 g (2 lb 6 oz)
Bicarbonate of soda	2.5 ml (1/2 tsp)	3.75 ml (3/4 tsp)	5 ml (1 tsp)	6.25 ml (1 1/4 tsp)	7.5 ml (1 1/2 tsp)	10 ml (2 tsp)	11.25 ml (2 1/4 tsp)	13.75 ml (2 3/4 tsp)
Baking powder	1.25 ml (1/4 tsp)	2.5 ml (1/2 tsp)	2.5 ml (1/2 tsp)	5 ml (1 tsp)	5 ml (1 tsp)	6.25 ml (1 1/4 tsp)	7.5 ml (1 1/2 tsp)	8.75 ml (1 3/4 tsp)
Eggs (medium)	3	3	4	5	6	8	9	11
Cooking time (approx.)	3/4 hr – 1 1/4 hrs	1 3/4 hrs – 2 1/4 hrs	1 3/4 hrs – 2 1/4 hrs	2 hrs – 2 1/2 hrs	2 1/4 hrs – 2 3/4 hrs	2 3/4 hrs – 3 1/4 hrs	3 1/4 hrs – 3 3/4 hrs	4 hrs – 4 1/2 hrs

INGREDIENTS INDEX

Almonds
(blanched, chopped, essence, flaked,
ground)
Apple Tea Bread   38
Chairman's Cake   18
Cherry Cake   27
Cherry and Almond Cake   28
Chocolate Almond Brownies   45
Christmas Cake   20
Coffee and Almond Cake   29
Dundee Cake   17
Fudgy Chocolate Loaf   50
Lemon and Ginger Cake   30
Macaroons   53
Mocha Cake   44
Modern Christmas Cake   20
Passion Cake   32
Peach and Almond Cake   37
Rich Almond Cake   31
Rich Chocolate Cake   50
Sandcake   33
Simnel Cake   22
Special Occasions Cakes   69

Amaretto liqueur
Peach and Almond Cake   37

Apples (cooking, eating)
Apple Tea Bread   38
Apple and Walnut Cake   15
Chairman's Cake   18
Mini Passion Cakes   57

Apricots (dried, ready-to-eat)
Apricot, Prune and Cherry Cake   16
Apricot and Coconut Bars   61
Cherry and Apricot Scones   60
Cranberry and Apricot Tea Bread   39
Modern Christmas Cake   20
Orange and Lemon Bars   61
Paradise Cake   15
Tropical Fruit Tea Loaf   42

Apricot jam
Rich Chocolate Cake   50
Sachertorte   52

Baking powder (throughout)

Bananas
Banana Butterscotch Cake   26
Banana Tea Loaf   39
Chocolate and Banana Cake   46

Bicarbonate of soda (throughout)

Blackcurrant jam
All-in-One Chocolate Cake   43

Blueberries (dried)
Modern Christmas Cake   20

Brandy
Boiled Fruit Cake   25
Christmas Cake   20
Half Pound Cake   24
Modern Christmas Cake   20
Simnel Cake   22
Special Occasions Cakes   69
Spiced Plum Tea Bread   41

Brazil Nuts
Chairman's Cake   18

Caraway seeds
Old Fashioned Seed Cake   28

Cardamom pods
Lemon and Cardamom Cake   29

Carrots
Mini Passion Cakes   57
Passion Cake   32

Cheese (full-fat soft)
Mini Passion Cakes   57

Cherries
Boiled Fruit Cake   25

Cherries (glacé)
Apricot, Prune and Cherry Cake   16
Banana Tea Loaf   39
Chairman's Cake   18
Cherry Cake   27
Cherry and Almond Cake   28
Cherry and Apricot Scones   60

INGREDIENTS INDEX

Christmas Cake   20
Date and Cherry Tea Loaf   40
Golden Christmas Cake   16
Half Pound Cake   24
Madeleines   56
Modern Christmas Cake   20
My Favourite Fruit Cake   14
Paradise Cake   15
Simnel Cake   22
Small Cakes   58
Snow White Cake   35
Special Occasions Cakes   68
Tea time Fruity Squares   62

Chocolate (dark, plain, bitter)
Chairman's Cake   18
Chocolate Almond Brownies   45
Chocolate and Banana Cake   46
Coconut and Chocolate Crunch   49
Death by Chocolate Fudge Cake   48
Mocha Cake   44
Orange Chocolate Drizzle Cake   46
Rich Chocolate Cake   50
Sachertorte   52
Small Cakes   58
Snow White Cake   35
Traditional American Brownies   51

Cinnamon
Coffee Pecan Bars   59
Modern Christmas Cake   20
Special Occasions Cakes   69
Spiced Honey Cake   34
Spiced Plum Tea Bread   41
Sticky Gingerbread   36
Tea time Fruity Squares   62

Cocoa powder (and drinking chocolate)
All-in-One Chocolate Cake   43
Chewy Chocolate Squares   44
Chocolate Cup Cakes   54
Coconut and Chocolate Crunch   49
Dark Chocolate Cake   47
Death by Chocolate Fudge Cake   48
Fudgy Chocolate Loaf   50
Light Chocolate Cake   49
Mini Passion Cakes   57
Moist Chocolate Cake   73

Snow White Cake   35
Swiss Roll (chocolate)   65
Traditional American Brownies   51

Coconut (desiccated)
Apricot and Coconut Bars   61
Coconut Buns   55
Coconut Cake   30
Coconut and Chocolate Crunch   49
Madeleines   56

Coffee (essence, instant, real)
Coffee and Almond Cake   29
Coffee Pecan Bars   59
Coffee and Walnut Cake   64
Mauritian Easter Cake   23
Mocha Cake   44
Sachertorte   52
Snow White Cake   35

Cornflour
Sandcake   33

Courgette
Marmalade and Courgette Cake   25

Cranberries
Apricot, Prune and Cherry Cake   16
Cranberry and Apricot Tea Bread   39
Modern Christmas Cake   20

Cream (double, single)
Death by Chocolate Fudge Cake   48
Mini Passion Cakes   57
Mocha Cake   44
Snow White Cake   35

Cream cheese
Banana Butterscotch Cake   26
Passion Cake   32

Cream (soured)
Death by Chocolate Fudge Cake   48

Cream of Tartar
Cherry and Apricot Scones   60
Scones   60

INGREDIENTS INDEX

Currants
Christmas Cake 20
Dundee Cake 17
Half Pound Cake 24
My Favourite Fruit Cake 14
Special Occasions Cakes 68

Dates
Date and Cherry Tea Loaf 40
Date and Walnut Cake 24
Date and Walnut Tea Bread 40

Drambuie
Chairman's Cake 18

Dried fruit (mixed)
Irish Tea Brack 23
Marmalade and Courgette Cake 25
Rock Cakes 58
Semi-Rich Fruit Cake 17
Simnel Cake 22

Eggs (throughout)

Figs (ready-to-eat)
Modern Christmas Cake 20

Flour (plain, self-raising, throughout)

Fromage frais
All-in-One Chocolate Cake 43

Fruit (mixed, fresh, dried)
Boiled Fruit Cake 25
Mixed Fruit Tea Loaf 42

Fruit salad
Boiled Fruit Cake 25
Sunshine Fruit Cake 21

Ginger (ground, stem, syrup)
Gingerbread Hollows 53
Lemon Butterfly Cakes 55
Lemon and Ginger Cake 30
Parkin 36
Simple Ginger Cake 32
Spiced Honey Cake 34
Sticky Gingerbread 36
Ginger Slice 62

Golden Syrup
Apricot and Coconut Bars 61
Date and Cherry Tea Loaf 40
Highland Fruit Cake 24
Lemon Butterfly Cakes 55
Lemon and Ginger Cake 30
Mixed Fruit Tea Loaf 42
Orange and Lemon Bars 61
Parkin 36

Guinness
Guinness Cake 19

Honey
Apple Tea Bread 38
Chairman's Cake 18
Golden Harvest Cake 18
Spiced Honey Cake 34

Lemon (juice, rind, zest)
Banana Butterscotch Cake 26
Christmas Cake 20
Cranberry and Apricot Tea Bread 39
Dundee Cake 17
Golden Harvest Cake 18
Lemon Butterfly Cakes 55
Lemon and Cardamom Cake 29
Lemon Drizzle Cake 31
Lemon and Ginger Cake 30
Madeira Cake 71
Marmalade and Courgette Cake 25
Old Fashioned Seed Cake 28
Orange and Lemon Bars 61
Paradise Cake 15
Passion Cake 32
Simnel Cake 22
Special Occasions Cakes 69
St Clement's Cake 37
Sunshine Fruit Cake 21

Lemon curd
Passion Cake 32

Mango (ready-to-eat)
Modern Christmas Cake 20

Marmalade (ginger)
Simple Ginger Cake 32

INGREDIENTS INDEX

Marmalade (lemon)
Marmalade and Courgette Cake   25

Marmalade (orange)
St Clement's Cake   37

Milk (variously)

Oatmeal
Parkin   36

Oats (rolled)
Apricot and Coconut Bars   61
Highland Fruit Cake   24
Orange and Lemon Bars   61

Orange (juice, syrup, zest)
Apricot and Coconut Bars   61
Apricot, Prune and Cherry Cake   16
Cranberry and Apricot Tea Bread   39
Mauritian Easter Cake   23
Modern Christmas Cake   20
Orange Chocolate Drizzle Cake   46
Orange and Lemon Bars   61
Rum and Orange Cake   34
Spiced Honey Cake   34

Papaya
Tropical Fruit Tea Loaf   42

Pastry, Shortcrust
Snow White Cake   35

Peaches
Peach and Almond Cake   37
Tropical Fruit Tea Loaf   42

Pears
Tropical Fruit Tea Loaf   42

Pecan nuts
Coffee Pecan Bars   59
Traditional American Brownies   51

Peel, mixed
Banana Tea Loaf   39
Christmas Cake   20
Dundee Cake   17

Guinness Cake   19
My Favourite Fruit Cake   14
Old Fashioned Seed Cake   28
Paradise Cake   15
Special Occasions Cakes   68
Sunshine Fruit Cake   21

Pineapple (dried, glacé, tinned)
Chairman's Cake   18
Golden Christmas Cake   16
Modern Christmas Cake   20
Paradise Cake   15
Sunshine Fruit Cake   21
Tropical Fruit Tea Loaf   42

Prunes
Apricot, Prune and Cherry Cake   16
Spiced Plum Tea Bread   41
Tropical Fruit Tea Loaf   42

Raisins
Chairman's Cake   18
Christmas Cake   20
Dundee Cake   17
Guinness Cake   19
Half Pound Cake   24
Mauritian Easter Cake   23
Orange and Lemon Bars   61
Special Occasions Cakes   68
Spiced Plum Tea Bread   41
Sunshine Fruit Cake   21

Raspberry jam (or alternative)
Madeleines   56
Raspberry Buns   56
Swiss Roll   65
Swiss Whirls   54

Rum
Mauritian Easter Cake   23
Rum and Orange Cake   34

Salt (occasionally)

Sherry
Coffee and Almond Cake   29
Golden Christmas Cake   16
Dundee Cake   17

INGREDIENTS INDEX

Spice (mixed)

Apple Tea Bread	38
Apple and Walnut Cake	15
Boiled Fruit Cake	25
Christmas Cake	20
Dundee Cake	17
Guinness Cake	19
Half Pound Cake	24
Highland Fruit Cake	24
Mini Passion Cakes	57
Mixed Fruit Tea Loaf	42
Modern Christmas Cake	20
Old Fashioned Seed Cake	28
Rock Cakes	58
Simnel Cake	22
Special Occasions Cakes	69
Spiced Plum Tea Bread	41

Sugar (demerara, golden caster, icing, molasses, muscovado light and dark, – throughout, variously)

Sultanas

Apple and Walnut Cake	15
Banana Tea Loaf	39
Christmas Cake	20
Dundee Cake	17
Golden Christmas Cake	16
Golden Harvest Cake	18
Guinness Cake	19
Half Pound Cake	24
Highland Fruit Cake	24
My Favourite Fruit Cake	14
Paradise Cake	15
Small Cakes	58
Special Occasions Cakes	68
Spiced Plum Tea Bread	41
Sunshine Fruit Cake	21
Tea time Fruity Squares	62

Sunflower oil

All-in-One Chocolate Cake	43

Sunflower seeds

Orange and Lemon Bars	61

Tea

Irish Tea Brack	23

Tia Maria

Coffee Pecan Bars	59
Mocha Cake	44
Sachertorte	52

Treacle (black)

All-in-One Chocolate Cake	43
Christmas Cake	20
Dark Chocolate Cake	47
Date and Cherry Tea Loaf	40
Date and Walnut Tea Bread	40
Mixed Fruit Tea Loaf	42
Parkin	36
Sticky Gingerbread	36

Vanilla essence

Chocolate and Banana Cake	46
Swiss Whirls	54
Death by Chocolate Fudge Cake	48

Walnuts

Apple and Walnut Cake	15
Banana Tea Loaf	39
Boiled Fruit Cake	25
Chairman's Cake	18
Chewy Chocolate Squares	44
Coffee and Walnut Cake	64
Date and Cherry Tea Loaf	40
Date and Walnut Cake	24
Date and Walnut Tea Bread	40
Golden Christmas Cake	16
Golden Harvest Cake	18
Guinness Cake	19
Half Pound Cake	24
Mini Passion Cakes	57
Paradise Cake	15
Passion Cake	32
Snow White Cake	35
Tropical Fruit Tea Loaf	42

ABOUT THE WI

If you have enjoyed this book, the chances are that you would enjoy belonging to the largest women's organisation in the country – the National Federation of Women's Institutes, or the WI as it is usually known.

We are friendly, go-ahead, like-minded women, who derive enormous satisfaction from all the movement has to offer. The list is long – you can make new friends, have fun and companionship, visit new places, develop new skills, take part in community services, fight local campaigns, become a WI Market producer, and play an active role in an organisation that has a national voice.

The WI is the only women's organisation in the country that owns an adult education establishment. At Denman College, you can take a course in anything from car maintenance to paper sculpture, from book binding to yoga, or cordon bleu cookery to fly fishing.

For more information, write to the **National Federation of Women's Institutes, 104 New Kings Road, London SW6 4LY, phone 0171-371-9300. The NFWI Wales Office is at 19 Cathedral Road, Cardiff CF1 9LJ, phone 01222-221712. For more information and a catalogue about WI Books, contact WI Books, Glebe House, Church Street, Crediton, Devon EX17 2AF, phone 01363 777575**

ABOUT THE AUTHOR

Jill Brand is currently the NFWI Home Economics Adviser, based at the NFWI Unit, Denman College. Her role is to give professional support and advice via the Home Economics Committee to Federations and Members on all aspects of Home Economics. She is a member of Bucknell WI, Oxfordshire.

Jill was previously employed in the domestic appliance industry where she was involved in design, development and testing of products to ensure the consumers' needs were met. She also developed, tested and wrote recipes for recipe books, leaflets and magazines as well as being involved in the production of consumer booklets.

Jill is a Fellow of the Institute of Home Economics.

In her spare time, she enjoys gardening, collecting antiques, reading and researching the history of food – and, of course, cooking.

BILLINGTONS
The Unrefined Sugar Experts

Edward Billington and Son Ltd is a family company which has imported sugar for over 140 years. The name of Billington is synonymous with the very best in brown and golden sugars.

Billington's sugar is the real thing!
Not all brown sugars are the same. Refined brown sugars are only brown on the outside; underneath they are really white sugar, which has been coated to add colour and some flavour.

Unrefined sugars are very simply produced with the aim of locking in – rather than refining out – the natural molasses of the sugar cane. It is this difference that gives unrefined sugar its superior flavour and natural colour to improve all your sweet and savoury dishes. As all good cooks know, the best results are produced using the finest ingredients – and when it comes to sugar, that means UNREFINED!

Billington's unrefined sugars are produced on the tropical island of Mauritius in the Indian Ocean. The natural sugar cane is simply shredded and crushed to press out the sugar juice. This juice is then clarified and crystallised to produce a wide range of golden, light and brown natural sugars.

There is an unrefined sugar for every type of recipe, and each has its own distinctive flavour and purpose. From **Golden Granulated** and **Organic Cane** sugars, the unrefined all-purpose alternatives to refined white sugar, to the rich, treacly taste of **Molasses** sugar – the only choice for enhancing the flavour of rich dark fruit cakes. The range of Billington sugars also includes **Sugar Crystals**, perfect for coffee or cake toppings, and a **Golden Icing Sugar** with a delicate buttery flavour and natural golden colour.

Unrefined sugars are available in all major supermarkets. To ensure you are buying the finest quality unrefined sugar, simply take a look on the packet for – **Unrefined** and **Produce of Mauritius.**

If you want to know more about Billington unrefined sugars, please contact us at **The Billington Food Group, Cunard Building, Liverpoool, L3 1EL. Tel: 0151-236-2265. Fax: 0151-236-2493,** visit our website at www.billingtons.co.uk or email us at bfg@billingtons.co.uk.

MORE FROM WI BOOKS

There are lots more books on cookery and crafts available from WI Books, the WI's own publishing company. WI Books publish and make available books of good value and special interest to WI members. There are many titles on Cooking, Crafts and Gardening, Painting and Drawing, as well as histories of the WI and of Denman College. A catalogue is available from WI Books, Glebe House, Church Street, Crediton, Devon EX17 2AF.

Prices for 1999 are shown for the following cookery titles selected from the list, and written by WI Members. These titles are also available to the general public. Contact WI Books at the address above or the distributor, Biblios, Star Road, Partridge Green, West Sussex RH13 8LD.

The new "WI Book of … " cookery series, tried and tested by WI Members:

Bread and Bakes	*Kay Bradley*	£4.95
Cooking for One	*Margaret Foss*	£4.95
Jams and Preserves	*Pat Hesketh*	£4.95
Salsas and Unusual Preserves	*Grace Mulligan*	£4.95
Sweets and Chocolates	*Clift, Green & Phillips*	£4.95
Vegetarian Cuisine	*Sîan Cook*	£4.95

Other titles available in the original series, tried and tested by WI Members:

Biscuits	£3.95	**Pastry**	£1.80
Fish and Seafood	£2.95	**Soups and Starters**	£2.95
Microwave Cookery	£2.95	**Vegetables and Salads**	£2.95

A Taste of WI Markets   *by WI Market Members*   £4.95

More than 135 recipes celebrate WI Markets' outstanding reputation as a source of fresh homemade cooking.

The Family Vegetarian   *by Mary Norwak*   £4.95

An extensive variety of delicious non-meat dishes with nutrition advice. For the family who want vegetarian meals within everyday cooking.

Simply Good Food   *by NFWI Wales*   £4.95

Over 130 recipes to make you feel well, look well and be well, using foods low in fat, salt and sugar, and high in fibre, to produce delicious and healthy food.